THE EDISON

A Life Tuned to the Unseen Laws

A Happy Thoughts Initiative

The Edison

A Life Tuned to the Unseen Laws

By WOW Publishings Pvt. Ltd., India

ISBN: 978-81-989258-3-1

Published by WOW Publishings Pvt. Ltd., India

First edition published in July 2025

Printed and bound by Trinity Academy
for Corporate Training Ltd, Pune

Facts Compiled by Terry Newman

To the original thinkers,
who bravely challenge the status quo,
and dedicate their lives to light
the path for human advancement.

Content

Preface
The Boy who Lit the World

What makes iconic figures in history so successful? Is it something in their DNA? Is it the fact that they received more "lucky breaks" than the average person? Or is there something more?

Thomas Alva Edison, in his lifetime, became an American folk hero. At the time of his passing in 1931, he had 1093 U.S. patents and 2332 patents worldwide—a record that stood for over 70 years. He is probably best known for his relentless work to bring to light the first commercially viable incandescent light bulb that made it possible to illuminate the entire world.

Edison is celebrated as one of history's most prolific and influential inventors of all time. During the late nineteenth and early twentieth century, his innovations fundamentally shaped modern life—from the telegraph to the phonograph to motion pictures to electricity. Perhaps no one else during that period did more to transform the American technological landscape.

It is the rarest of rare occurrences to witness someone who could not only innovate but also work to bring the innovation into the world for mainstream consumption. His laboratory at Menlo Park became the world's first industrial research laboratory. Here, he pioneered the use of teamwork and organized scientific inquiry in the invention process, into a system that could be blueprinted and used anywhere. Most people marvel at this feat but very few question how exactly he could accomplish so much in a lifetime.

If, up to this point, you have come to believe that such feats are possible only for a lucky few endowed with qualities coming from divine intervention or being born as freaks of nature, his very ordinary beginnings are going to surprise you. Also, Edison is not known to have explicitly been a follower of any philosophical or religious tenets for his success. He was a man who took action and then duplicated his actions when they met with success. He did this on a scientific level with an instinct that comes with experience and deep observation.

Edison made it a point to take time out of his day and spend it in solitude on a regular basis. Did he formally meditate? It is not known. He did, however, advocate spending time alone and listening to the inner voice. He instinctively understood that there were unseen laws at work to bring about any result. To quote his own words:

"I know this world is ruled by infinite intelligence. Everything that surrounds us—everything that exists—proves that there

are infinite laws behind it. There can be no denying this fact. It is mathematical in its precision."

Just as there are laws governing the physical world, there are laws governing the mental world as well. This book is an effort to look at Edison's life from the perspective of these unseen laws that worked to bring results for him at various stages of his life.

These are the *Laws of Thought* as described in the book, *The Source ... Power of Happy Thoughts* by Sirshree. Edison's life experiences are explained in the light of these fundamental principles. Each of these principles have been brought to light through instances from Edison's life. The passages that follow provide insights about how to align your life to the *Law of Creation*, the *Law of Focus*, or the *Law of Integrity*, to make them work for you. You'll learn about the *Law of Abundance in Nature* and how you can tap into it to eliminate any lack in your life. The *Law of Influence* assures you that you can be in total control of your own destiny. Also, you'll see how the *Law of Resonance* can bring clarity in how you perceive the world and how you can change it.

Within each of us resides a wellspring of potential. By aligning with these powerful laws, we can be the best that we were meant to be—whatever our calling may be. As you delve into Edison's journey, keep an eye out for the understanding behind how the laws work. All the laws are presented in the context of real-life situations, and hence it becomes easier to digest and internalize them.

There is no substitute for contemplation in the context of your own situation. Hence, pause to contemplate on what is working for you and cement its conviction. Observe what is not working for you, the mistakes that could possibly be happening, and rectify them. Use the insights that dawn on you to craft your destiny.

Editors' Note

While I was compiling, editing and working with the Happy Thoughts Research wing on this book, more than one person in my circle asked me about how Edison could possibly have employed the Laws of Thought when he probably was only more focused on scientific laws.

I replied simply with a question of my own. "Are you a scientist?"

Of course, the answer was always no. "You use scientific laws every day, like the law of gravity. Yet, you claim not to be a scientist."

The truth of the matter is that the Laws of Thought are at work for all of us, whether we realize they exist or not. The fact that some of us are aware of them is a bonus. That means we can leverage them to our fullest advantage.

In fact, the same laws apply to those who seek material success, scientific success, social success, or even spiritual success. Whatever you call these laws, they work the same for everyone, whether one believes they exist or not. The key is that you have to work within to align with them till they become your internal framework, after which they automatically work to your advantage.

The laws worked for Edison because he instinctively aligned to them. He may have approached at least some of these laws much like he did his experiments. Some other laws may have worked for him without him being conscious of them, since all these laws are intricately connected.

The scientific world isn't going to verify results if the consequences are found in one isolated experiment. Researchers and other scientists need to get the same results consistently before they see a law or principle forming.

Nevertheless, they worked for Edison, and now, it is your turn to take these principles, tested, retested and verified by one of the greatest innovative minds in history, and to see them work for you.

- *Terry Newman*

This book is an initiative of the 'Happy Thoughts' research wing. One of the focus areas of this wing is to highlight biographies of inspirational personalities, who illustrate the great values that their lives epitomized. The intent is to bring forth what it was in the fabric of their character that made these personalities stand out and inspire the world. Thus, in the process, provide working principles for every person to emulate.

- *Happy Thoughts Research Wing*

Disclaimer

This book is not intended to be a complete biography of Thomas Alva Edison. It is meant to illustrate how the potent Laws of Thought propelled the inventor to success.

While the major facts of Edison's life are accurate, the editors have taken the liberty to build in dialogue, which may or may not have occurred. Such dialogues are intended to help illustrate a point and to make it a more engaging reading experience. It in no way changes the facts of Edison's life or the truth of the Source laws at work.

A Note on The Electric Bulb

It may also be pertinent here to break a misconception in this area. Popular notion tends to project Edison as the inventor of the electric bulb. It must be acknowledged however that incandescent lighting existed for decades before him as a scientific development in labs with several breakthrough inventions of its components. However, thanks to Edison's relentless efforts, it got transformed into the first commercially viable, long-lasting system for electric lighting.

1

The Not-so-obvious Signs of a Genius

You'd imagine that such a success story would start out with the image of a young boy, precocious in every way, bright beyond his years, with all the adults marveling at his innate inventiveness. You could imagine that. You would not, however, be describing the early childhood years of Edison.

Certain events of his life are already well known and quite true… He was born in Milan, Ohio as the youngest of the seven children of Samuel and Nancy Elliott Edison. Four of them survived childhood, and he was one of them. But his siblings were at least 15 years elder to him. So, at his time, he was the only child in the house.

His father was an exiled Canadian political activist and his mother was an accomplished teacher. The traits, that Edison would be renowned for as an adult, could surely be seen in the actions and practices of his parents.

Those of Edison's biographers, who studied his parents, provide detailed characteristics that Al, as he was known in his family, would carry with him throughout his life. His dad, Samuel, had been involved in the Mackenzie Rebellion of 1837 in Ontario, Canada, inspired by the democratic activist, William Mackenzie. The revolt, however, failed. Samuel found he could no longer live in that country and migrated to the United States. And it was here that he made his home.

In the middle to late nineteenth century, the United States witnessed what would eventually be called the Industrial Revolution. This time period proved to be a good match for Edison's father. He tapped into his entrepreneurial spirit, working on a series of ventures.

He would start projects. If they didn't succeed, it didn't matter. He would then view the problem from a different angle, from another perspective; he'd simply set that idea aside and continue on to another. No regrets. No judgments.

You can be sure, though, that he took away lessons to be applied to his next project. All this time, his young son, Al, as his parents called him, was watching how he handled his life.

It is known that attitudes can be passed through DNA to some extent. However, it is established that observation and nurturing play a far more significant role, though less apparent to outsiders. DNA can define inclinations, but observation and internalization refine the act to generate deeper, quality outcomes.

This trait was transferred to young Al. He brought the same spirit, persistence, and determination to all of his inventions, projects, and businesses. It was as if failure were not a part of his vocabulary.

His mother was a talented and accomplished individual in her own right, something that most women of the early nineteenth century could not say for themselves. The daughter of a well-known Presbyterian minister and the granddaughter of a revolutionary war hero, she was trained as a teacher. Her background and beliefs, as well as her secular training, would serve Al well as he matured.

Young Al didn't speak until age 4

His parents could tell that Al's development, even as an infant, didn't conform to a typical childhood narrative. From this rocky beginning, no one—with the exception of his mother—could have predicted the amazing accomplishments that lie in his future.

Perhaps the lad's development and later his behavior as a preschooler should have served as signals to the family that their son did not conform to the world's standards. And perhaps it did. No one has written what his parents thought. The fact that Al didn't begin to talk until he was four years old could have given his mom and dad reason to be concerned about the proper development of their son.

There is certainly no way to tell if they had intimate conversations about their son's development, or the apparent lack of it, in the silence of the late night when young Al was safely tucked into bed. However, one thing that seems certain is that as he grew and matured, they never treated him as a child who may have learning problems.

It would have been easy enough for Samuel and Nancy Edison to begin worrying or having negative thoughts about their son, Al, who did not speak until he was four years old. Undoubtedly, well-meaning friends and family members questioned them about it.

One can only suppose that his parents took these questions and any suggestions from others about dealing with the situation in their stride. Al's inability or refusal to talk was something that friends and family may have discussed, even if they didn't include Nancy and Samuel in their conversations.

How easy it could have been for his parents to envision grim outcomes. But it doesn't appear to have happened so. They seemed to have treated him no differently from any of their other children, who had no issues with talking in their tender years.

The Law of Influence

Others' thoughts cannot influence you unless you allow them to.

Explanation

You should care about your own thoughts, as they are the only thing in your control. You should introspect your thoughts and choose them wisely. The most influential factor in your life is your own thoughts. If you understand this, nothing will adversely affect you, even when interacting with people who have a negative mindset. Be aware and vigilant to avoid being swayed when you are listening to negative chatter.

If you fear that other's thoughts about you are negative and their thoughts about you will turn to reality, then let go of this fear. When travelling in a bus, there may be twenty who might fear an accident. But what matters is the confidence of the driver. If he is positive and unfazed, the bus will reach its destination safely and smoothly. If you are positive and the driver isn't, then you won't be on that bus. So, either way, there is nothing to fear, and there is only one place to act – within yourself.

While the *Law of Creation* implies that everything is first created in the dimension of thoughts, the Law of Influence is a safeguard. It means that only your own thoughts affect creation in your life. Also, you cannot adversely affect anyone else's life unless their thoughts are influenced by your interactions with them.

Al's parents were aligning with the Law of Influence, regardless of whether they were aware of it. They refused to judge their son's abilities based on others' opinions or conventional behavior. Outer behavior made people believe that the preschooler had some type of disability. But they knew enough about life and human behavior to be convinced that Al's silence was not due to disability. If his parents even considered this for a moment, they never acted upon it. They did not let others' opinions about their son influence their understanding and therefore, did not project these onto their son's thoughts and beliefs about himself.

We can now imagine how they envisioned their son, day after day, as talking and succeeding in the world despite how others may have thought or felt about this. Both Nancy and Samuel knew, at their core, that their thoughts and beliefs had power. That included any thoughts they may have projected onto Al.

Edison's parents treated him as an intelligent child who simply had not spoken yet. Nature is inherently positive and has a progressive plan for each one of us. However, we must align with this plan and trust it.

You know how this vignette of Al's life turned out. He did start talking around the age of four. Ironically, once he started speaking, there was really no holding him back.

It would be helpful here to review our own life to check where we've been judging ourselves or others by external appearances. Have we allowed conventional labels to dictate how we see ourselves or others. It is worth questioning our perspectives.

On the question of not speaking for long, it is often seen that you observe more intensely and listen more intently when you do not speak. Who knows whether young Al was sharpening his faculties of observation and deeper inference during this phase when he hardly spoke!

Natural curiosity

Marion, Al's older sister, was married to Homer Page. Homer was a farmer. Al often visited his sister during holidays. He used to spend a lot of time in the fields where he would watch the ducks in the farm for hours.

"Al...Al...Thomas... where are you?", Homer shouted as he kept climbing the small green hill. He was searching for little Al. Spotting Al standing near the ducks on the farm, with his feet covered with yellow egg yolk, Homer wondered what he was up to.

"What are you doing, Al? Look at yourself." Homer began cleaning Al's clothes as he inquired.

"I sat on those duck eggs," Al replied.

"Why were you sitting on them?" Homer asked with curiosity.

"I noticed that when hens and ducks sit on eggs, chicks emerge. But when I sat, the eggs broke and soiled my clothes. Why did this happen?" Al enquired.

Homer burst into laughter. "Al, you are small, but I love the way you think and the sharpness of your brain. I know why this happened. But for now, let's go home quickly. Your sister has been waiting for you."

When Al got home, Marion heaved a sigh of relief. But she saw that Al was sad. Homer shared the story of Al's failed experiment with eggs.

She consoled Al, "You tried well, Al. It does not matter if you failed. If one stops experimenting, one will never learn anything. Keep up your experiments, and you will eventually discover how it all works."

Al took his sister's advice to heart and never stopped experimenting. This incident from his childhood gives us a glimpse of his inquisitive nature.

There was, indeed, no stopping young Al from talking – more specifically questioning – once he did begin to talk. Most of his time was spent questioning every adult he met about nearly everything under the sun. He wanted to know how everything worked.

As you can well expect, many adults would have had to confess that they didn't know the inner workings of many things. And if they told the boy they didn't know, his next question for them would be, "Why?" Why don't you know?"

This continual questioning of everything would not abate even when he entered school, which was not a trait that endeared him to his grade school instructor.

2

Orthodox Schooling

His instructor, Rev. E.B. Engle, taught young Al and 37 other youngsters in a one-room schoolhouse. He had no time to cater to the overly inquisitive young mind of Edison. At least, that's the way the instructor saw it.

The school system, moreover, had recently adopted the Prussian style of education. This required rote memorization, and for the most part, complete silence from the students. Whatever knowledge the children needed to know at this age would be funneled their way at the right moments and through the proper channels, meaning the teacher. This meant that Al could not ask questions at random.

This didn't jibe with Al's natural inclination to learn through experimentation and asking questions – a myriad of questions. But those weren't the only strikes the teacher was racking up against the lad. Sure, his questions interrupted class, but his instructor also considered him to have an "addled" brain.

Edison tended to ramble from one topic that interested him to another in what seemed like lightning speed. Clearly, his teacher concluded, the child was hyperactive. In today's school environment, he would easily be labeled as having Attention Deficient Disorder and hence would be recommended to be placed on a prescription drug for the disorder. He continued to ask questions instead of sitting quietly and waiting to be told what he needed to learn.

But even worse, in the mind of his teacher were other disturbing traits of Edison. Being a shy boy, he had trouble expressing himself verbally in front of others. His instructor was also convinced the lad would never be able to write either.

And about his performance in mathematics, his instructor assumed that this was beyond the boy's capability. The young boy was doomed to be hindered at every level of his learning, according to the instructor. The teacher additionally detested the fact that he would daydream—at least that appeared to be what the boy was doing. Whatever he was doing, one thing was for certain: Edison was not paying attention to the classroom curriculum.

The school instructor, out of frustration, even found it necessary to comment on the shape and size of Al's head to prove his point, noting that it was larger than most children and misshapen. This, in his teacher's mind, only illustrated even more clearly, that Edison had no future career in that school.

Young Al drops out

If you read the stories about this short but impressionable twelve-week period in Al's life, you're told that his mother withdrew him from school, which she eventually did. But it was actually young Al who initiated her confrontation with his instructor.

Or perhaps it would be more apt to say that he avoided a confrontation. He simply walked out of the schoolroom one day and went home after taking as much of the name-calling as he could stand. The following day, his mother escorted him to school. Instead of making the young man apologize for his actions, she defended her son. Of course, in the process, she condemned the actions of the instructor and the treatment her son had received from him.

No one really knows what was said in that classroom on that day, but it's likely that Mrs. Edison set about to give the instructor, supposedly a spiritual man himself, a lecture on the laws of life.

"Rev. Engle," she may have said, "Are you not a man of God?"

"You know very well I am, Mrs. Edison," he replied. It looked as if he was enraged at the question.

"No, sir, I do not," she said tersely. Before he had a chance to say anything, she continued. "What I do know is that you use the title of 'Reverend' more as a shield to protect yourself from criticism and blame. I don't see you using it as an instrument of God's love."

"I don't know what you're talking about, Mrs. Edison," Rev. Engle said.

"I mean you're holding the entire class hostage with your name-calling and your belittling them," she said. "You're doing it to my son Al, for one. You're limiting their potential with this despicable action."

She waited a beat, but before Rev. Engle could think quickly enough to give her an answer, she continued. "It's come to my attention you believe my son's brains arc 'addled', isn't that the phrase you used, sir?"

"He can't seem to concentrate on anything for more than few minutes," he answered quickly, in defense of his actions.

Nancy folded her arms. The tapping of her toe echoed throughout the schoolroom, which became disturbingly quiet as all the children sat mesmerized by the interaction of the two adults.

Rev. Engle continued, "He shows no evidence of having any mathematical ability."

"He has not yet displayed these traits," Edison's mom corrected him. "That does not mean he is incapable of performing arithmetic. For the moment, he perhaps chooses not to. Labeling him as ignorant in arithmetic, however, will hinder him throughout the rest of his formal education as well as his adulthood."

"There's no evidence to support that he'll ever learn arithmetic..."

Mrs. Edison stopped him midsentence, "There is no evidence that says he can't or won't eventually learn arithmetic, is there Rev. Engle?"

"W-why… uhm…" he began.

Then Al's mom quickly strode over to another young man in the room, her black shoes clicking on the floor. "I understand you've also labeled young Johnny Carney here as 'addled' as well."

"He cannot seem to grasp any scientific facts longer than a few moments," Rev. Engle said.

Mrs. Edison sighed, "If you continue to label these children this way, not one of them will believe they have any talent. Not one of them will go on to discover their potential."

She paused another moment, then continued, "While there are some individuals who may not realize what they are doing when they judge others by the appearances of their actions, but for you, Rev. Engle, it should be considered a sin.

"Don't you know that thoughts tend to attract similar thoughts? For example, the more you think of young Johnny here as being poor in science, the more attention and energy is given to that thought, regardless of whether it's the truth or not. Johnny, if told enough, will begin to believe it himself."

It was at this point that Mrs. Edison, stopped and whispered something in his ear. "Similarly, the more you chastise my son for being addled-brained, the more he'll come to believe it himself. Rev. Engle, we are dealing with my son's future. I cannot allow your ignorance to limit his potential.

"I cannot allow anyone to think of him as anything less than a smart, ambitious young man, destined for great things. His inability to stay on topic, I view as alacrity of his mind. His mind is quickly sizing up the situation and its inherent issues. It's not because he's addled that he doesn't stay with one subject. It's because he has swiftly assessed what he needs from that topic.

"Every single student in here is a gift from God," Mrs. Edison continued, "and I should know, I spent enough years teaching young minds just like this. Only where you see nothing but dismal failures, I see a classroom of bright young minds ready to ask questions and learn everything they could.

"And because of your failure to be positive, I am taking my child out of your classroom and making sure he gets the proper unlimited education his mind deserves."

Mrs. Edison turned on her heel, Al quickly followed, and she marched toward the door. Before she reached the exit, though, she heard cheers and applause. She glanced backward to see the children giving her a standing ovation.

When the mother and son were out of the room and the door was securely closed, young Edison said, "Why Mother, I do believe Rev. Engle may have an addled brain, himself."

Indeed, Nancy Elliot Edison had the credentials to do exactly what she said she would—remove her son from that toxic environment, from the angle of both academic and life's lessons.

Al's mother innately saw beyond appearances. She knew that if he stayed in school and continually had to listen to this man call him "stupid" month after month, Al himself would begin to view himself as stupid. Even more importantly, once he was labeled as being stupid, that stigma would continue further.

The instructor was the only teacher in that one-room schoolhouse. It was likely he would have been the only instructor Al had in his elementary school years. That meant he would have heard the negative talk not only month in and month out, but year in and year out!

According to the Law of Resonance, external circumstances are not what they appear to be, but a reflection of one's internal mind makeup. There was a distinct possibility that by being trained with a low self-esteem, Al would end up creating a world around him that resonated this negativity. That would have caused the greatest damage to him and his potential.

Through instinct and keen observation, she recognized the mental capacity of her son. She would have constantly uplifted her son's intelligence, and indeed his entire being, so he would grow up and live to his potential. She knew instinctively that she could save him from being stuffed into a mold that he had no reason to be in.

There is evidence that she clearly saw something extraordinary in his abilities. On his mother deciding to homeschool him and how she communicated the same to him, Edison says that *she was the making of him.* He narrates how, when she pulled him out of school, she mentioned a letter from the school that he was a child with the capabilities of a genius and that they did not have the adequate capabilities to feed his genius.

Many years later, after she had passed, he discovered the real letter which had actually said the opposite – that he was mentally deficient and hence could not attend school. What a turnaround her belief in him being a *genius* did to his life! The whole world looks up to him even today.

3

Unorthodox Schooling

For those times, it was indeed an unorthodox education. In fact, today, few young people receive an opportunity to learn as Al Edison did. And compared to today, it was of extremely short duration.

Most biographers recognize that from the time his mother took him out of school at age seven to the time he reached the age of eleven, she didn't follow a typical lesson plan or syllabus. Instead, she allowed his interests to dictate the direction of his education. In a very real way, mother and son became true partners in his schooling.

As psychologist Dr. Lucy Jo Palladino, explained about Nancy Edison's actions, "She made a deliberate decision to define her son by his strengths, not his weaknesses."

The Law of Focus

Focus on what you want, not what you don't want.

Explanation

This law is the working principle of the results you see in your life. *What you describe is what gets prescribed in your life.* If you are ill and your description of the situation is the symptoms of the illness, it will continue to repeat and persist in your life. Instead, if during an illness, you take it as a reminder to define what you want – perfect and vibrant health – then that is the direction your focus will work towards. Because, *wherever attention goes, energy flows.*

In Al's case the focus remained on his genius and his focus was directed toward opening up that potential. Had his mother rued on the misquotes on his abilities by his previous school and how unjust they were, young Al would certainly have gravitated to becoming a complaining personality. Thank God for it not happening so. Instead, his focus lay on experimenting and understanding how things worked and directing all his energies to becoming an innovator par excellence.

Young Al responded and reciprocated his mother's trust and guidance. He soaked up all the learning he could. Between her and his father, they steered the lad toward some of the best classic novels up to that time.

At times, Al read faster than his parents could supply them to him. While very often Nancy is given full credit for Al's home-school education, his father also played a vital role.

It was his father who would encourage his son to read the classics and world history – even if it meant "bribing" him.

Samuel Edison would reward Al with a dime for every classic book he read. Al rose to the challenge, reading such books as Gibbons' *The Decline and Fall of the Roman Empire.*

He was indeed becoming what his parents had envisioned he could be – an inquisitive, learned, young lad. He acquired a deep and abiding love for literature and poetry as part of this unique education. This side of his education surprises many. His favorite poetry was Grey's *Elegy in a Country Churchyard.* He memorized it as a child and even as an adult could be heard reciting portions of it in his workroom.

The Law of Focus at work

It was in these early years of his education that we can see the Law of Focus at work. When you begin to think in positive terms about any situation, more positive energy flows to the situation. The more persistently you hold your desired life in thought, the greater the likelihood of encountering perfectly aligned events and circumstances.

Nancy Edison schooled him for four years as she intensively directed his focus. She flooded her consciousness, as well as his, with uplifting thoughts. She held him in high esteem. She visualized him as learning and learning quickly. And she saw the great potential he held.

Additionally, she knew that it was merely a matter of divine timing before Al would see it too. She was right. He was beginning to recognize his own potential. He not only read these books, but also at times, questioned them. The power of questioning the authorities could only occur in an environment that was friendly, supportive, and free of judgment. Undoubtedly, that was just the environment Nancy and Samuel Edison provided for their son.

The Law of Focus works purely for oneself, and it is not possible for us to influence another, unless the other is ready to be influenced. This is the Law of Influence that was discussed earlier.

Young children are naturally receptive and impressionable. Hence, they have to be treated with utmost care. One never knows what inadvertent remark or behavior, their trusting child would take in, and in what manner. In case of Al, his parents were full of positivity, and he lapped up this positivity to enhance his capabilities.

So many negative influences existed in his childhood due to his unusual learning behavior. But what mattered finally is whom he believed in the most. To him, his mother's words were the gospel. Lucky that she shielded all the negative thoughts that could have had devastating effects on his psyche. Instead, she converted them to his advantage.

As you grow up and mature and learn to form your own independent opinions only after carefully assessing opinions that are thrown at you, you are on safer grounds.

The second part of Edison's education

By the time Al turned 11, his parents had nearly exhausted the resources of even their well-stocked library and taught him how to use the public library. Not having any idea of what lay ahead of him, Al thought an effective strategy to conquering the books of the library would be to read them, one by one.

He decided he would take a section of the racks and simply read one book after another as they were already placed on the library shelves. Certainly, he had a strategy, but his parents recognized it wasn't a very effective one.

His dad, quite wisely, steered him toward the more well-written and elevated books of the day. Within one short year, by the age of twelve, Al had far surpassed the reading list of the typical twelve-year old. He had read Sears' *History of the World* and Burton's *Anatomy of Melancholy.*

His education took a surprise twist, at least for his mother. She discovered that he was most in his element when he was lost in science books. He read with the greatest interest *The World Dictionary of Science* as well as several works on practical chemistry.

A year earlier, he had already set up a chemistry laboratory in his parents' basement. It was here that he practiced and honed his love, appreciation, and skill of practical chemistry.

While they were delighted with his interest in this area, they also realized they weren't capable of helping him advance in it. They themselves knew very little. There was one question in particular which completely opened his parents' eyes to their inability to aid him in focusing his interests in this direction.

Al read Isaac Newton's original work, *Principia*. They could not answer even his simplest questions about this renowned work. They were not wealthy, but they found the money to hire a tutor to aid Al in understanding the complex mathematical principles and style of Isaac Newton.

Even at this tender age, the budding scientist in his own right had distinct views on Newton's treatise. He disliked the way the principles were stated, feeling the language kept the average layperson from thoroughly understanding them.

It was as if, he thought, the realm of this knowledge was purposely being hidden from the common individual. His knee-jerk reaction led him to a life-long rejection and dislike of not only what he called "high-tone" language, but the subject of mathematics in general.

But there were elements of Newton's classic work that Edison appreciated, and that was the pure science itself. The simple beauty of Newton's laws struck him. But he looked at them not so much for their innate exquisiteness, but more for the fact that—even at this young age—he could learn from them.

He opened his mind to the creativity inherent in science, and when he did, Nature rewarded him with even more questions and ideas – something that would be a hallmark of his entire life.

From the moment he read Newton's laws, it is said that he adopted these as a standard to follow in developing his own unique style of verifying his theories. Up until this point, he had what could only be called a "freewheeling" style of thinking. Given how young he was, his desire to modify, improve, and purposefully mature his reasoning is quite impressive and, no doubt, a move that reveals wisdom beyond his years. It also displays the maturity of acceptance and an embrace of the creative process.

Once he read and realized the depths of Newton's theories, he then was able to develop his own set of logical steps for verifying his ideas and concepts. This, indeed, is not a decision that every ten- or eleven-year-old makes on his own. A key factor in his unconventional approach was the freedom from mental barriers that often accompany traditional schooling. Unlike many, for whom education becomes a passive obligation, learning was deeply and wholeheartedly integrated into his life. One of the most powerful laws was at work here – the Law of Integrity.

The Law of Integrity

Align your feelings, thoughts, words and actions to achieve your highest potential.

Explanation

When what you feel is what you think, what you think is what you speak, and what you speak is what you do, then all these four aspects are in alignment, effectively enabling you to manifest what you aspire to. That's why it is so very important that what you are involved in be the same as your interest.

The lessons Al gleaned from Newton's Principia also made him keenly aware that he could selectively collect lessons from other legendary scientists as well.

Edison's views of himself

No biographer of Edison mentions this, but this juncture may well be the critical turning point for the young scientist. Indeed, he was coming into his own as a scientist the moment he realized he needed to develop a dependable system upon which to base his observations and his hypotheses.

His thorough reading of Newton's Principia also made him question the reason for the style of the writing of the treatise. Edison resented what he saw as an excessively ornate and cryptic style. In his eyes these thoughts could have been written in a simpler manner. If it had, many more may have benefited from this knowledge.

Another insight he took from reading the great scientists was that sometimes their own preconceived notions limited their ability to view their work from what he would consider the proper perspective. He felt that many, in fact, were entrenched in a dogma—and it really didn't matter what type—that stymied their thoughts. Once their thoughts were stilted in any way, their research would automatically be inhibited, preventing them from seeing all the many possibilities.

At this point in his life, Edison was already taking the material lessons, learning from them and looking beyond to see the unseen principles at work. He was aware that all things were possible. Even at his age, he could see that some of the greatest scientists subconsciously limited their own learning by placing obstacles in their path.

Edison knew that he needed to come to science with a clean slate, an open mind, so to speak, and believe in his heart that truly anything was possible. He definitely made a personal vow not to allow himself to be tied to dogma. Once he opened himself up to this type of thinking, success couldn't be far behind.

It was at this point that he allowed creativity to flow through him. It is a law of Nature that once you're receptive to any creative idea, then you become a channel through which more and greater creative ideas flow. Did you ever notice that certain individuals seem to be brimming with creative ideas? That's because they allowed one to enter and automatically opened themselves up to more.

There's no way of knowing what Edison was thinking through these years. All we can do is observe the material he read and try to extrapolate from the actions he took. One thing we can be sure of, though, is that he entered his scientific studies with as open a mind as anyone could. And that is a prerequisite for success.

Al was only taking the preliminary steps toward discovering his potential. He still had a lifetime ahead of him.

But there's still another piece of the puzzle to place in this picture. Assuming that all you need to do is to think positive – and poof! – the solution appears magically, may have misled you. Blind following is never a workable solution… the moment you do this you miss out on the power of these laws. But as you gain insight into the Source laws, you will see the need for the Law of Integrity to be joined in. Your efforts will gain more intensity and purpose and then you will actually begin to see the results.

There is one quality needed to bring all the laws to fruition – continuity with regularity. It is really a combination of persistence and consistency. Once you set your sights on a goal, you, then, need to take the necessary steps. You need to persistently continue, step after step, no matter what the external circumstances, the appearances, indicate or how much of the outcome is visible.

An example of persistence is a person hammering away at a stone to break it. If the stone were to break after 100 blows, then the first 99 of them have to be persisted with. They are not a wasted effort, no matter what the visible outcome is at each stage. Consistency (where you introduce a kind of a pattern or frequency) is doing a little at a time but performing this pattern with a devout regularity.

This is the most difficult aspect for the mind to accept. It expects immediate results or wants to achieve big things at the very beginning. But the secret is that the habit of doing that little bit at a time, day in and day out, one day brings about a transformation so great that you find it hard to believe. This is the reason there is great awe and surprise at big achievements. The consistent and persistent effort behind the final achievement gets hidden. People attribute these achievements to talent or gifted personalities. The sustained effort behind attaining the state of spontaneity is never seen.

Edison's life is an epitome of this quality. You will see this throughout the book. There was no trace of lethargy in his life, either mental or physical. The readiness for any amount of effort that he had to put on a project is rarely seen in many other disillusioned aspirants of success. Note here the term "readiness." It is not the case that one *struggles* with effort. You will put in the required effort easily without it being a struggle. Because of your single-mindedness towards your goal and your complete involvement, this effort will take place naturally.

The Source laws work, and this is an assurance beyond doubt. But let's be aware of times when we lose focus of the goal. Then there is a danger of the laws being stated as an excuse for lethargy.

4

Telegraphy, Telephony, and Much More

Armed with what he felt was a sufficient amount of knowledge of the world around him—and no doubt, eager to learn more—Edison convinced his parents he was ready to enter the working world at the tender age of twelve. Although, in those times, a growing number of children went off to work in factories at this age or even younger, it could not have been an easy decision for his parents to make.

But it did, in some ways represent a giant victory for Al. Considering that he did not speak until he was four and his school-teacher found him inept in expressing himself during the short time of the formal educational stint, this was probably no small feat. His alignment and adherence to the laws of Nature paid off. He had acquired the level of confidence and self-belief that is needed even before one contemplates such a step.

Edison's parents did not view him as the world did. It is only fair to imagine they would not have agreed to this if they felt their son were not ready.

He began modestly. Al's first job on the railroad was selling candy, cigarettes and other items to the passengers on the train. And he was successful at it. Thanks to his keen mind and inquisitive nature, he saw an opportunity to take what was there in plain sight and turn it into a unique money-making opportunity.

What was there was a relatively new invention—thanks to the technological revolution of his time—the telegraph. Using this newly developed form of communication, data and information were able to travel cross-country faster than ever before, within minutes in fact.

The telegraph as an invention was less than 30 years old, and its uses were still being discovered. Each train station was equipped with a teletype machine. For a long time, this machine was the fastest way to send news bulletins to others, even across the country; and also, the fastest way to receive, what would be at that time, the very latest up-to-date news from all over.

One of the innovations the telegraph spawned was the rise of news associations. They had reporters nationwide—and later worldwide—and could actually supply its readers with up to the minute accounts of the news. Edison recognized the importance of these, even in his pre-teen years.

He acquired a small printing press and the necessary typesetting supplies. He then talked the stationmaster into allowing him access to the teletype machine. Additionally, the stationmaster allowed him to sell the paper, which he called *The Grand Trunk Herald*, inside the train itself.

Not surprisingly, the railroad passengers loved the idea of getting the very latest news and being able to read it on their ride. It was also fortuitous timing on Edison's part. The country was fascinated with the ongoing presidential debates between Abraham Lincoln and Steven Douglass.

This venture marked the first of what would be a long line of entrepreneurial ventures for him. This foray into the newspaper business vividly illustrates his ability to view circumstances from a different angle. But more than that, he was amenable to developing an inspired idea from what he saw.

Essentially, Edison saw the same thing every other employee of the train station saw, but was able to piece it together in order to solve a need. Edison inherently employed the Law of Creation to begin his first enterprise.

The Law of Creation

Before anything is created in the physical plane, it is first created from the Source in the mental plane.

Explanation

This means, the first creation happens when an idea or a concept arises from the Source through an individual. Depending on what you are open for and tuned to, the idea or thought occurs in your mind, originating from the Source. The second creation then follows when one manifests the idea as a material object or condition in the physical or visible plane.

This is exactly what young Edison did with his newspaper enterprise. The concept is no different for you today than it was for Edison. You too can create anything you need or want. First, secure it firmly and vividly in your mind with clarity and purpose. Then the Law of Manifestation comes into play.

The Law of Manifestation

When you direct thoughts consciously and passionately, they manifest.

Explanation

This means you should reflect and contemplate on your idea from all angles and clear and eliminate all doubts. Bring about clarity in intention so that the intention does not waver. Passion will automatically follow. Now just look at how things happen and fall in place—including your own involvement—in the process of its manifestation.

Edison's chemical laboratory

Never one to idle away time, Edison also took advantage of his free time with his new duties. He set up a small chemical lab in one of the train baggage cars. However, this idea did not end well.

The train was traveling an especially bumpy section of track on a particular day. In response, the train lurched.

This caused a stick of phosphorous to roll onto the floor of the train car that housed Edison's chemical set. A fire erupted, causing the baggage car to burn.

The conductor who rushed in to try to extinguish the fire was so irate that he struck Edison along the side of the head. This was a common and acceptable form of discipline in the day, called boxing of the ears. But it was not an act that was without its physical complications.

The boxing apparently caused a further injury to the young man's already impaired hearing. It's said that when he was younger, Edison contracted scarlet fever that left him with impaired hearing by the time he was fourteen.

Whatever the cause, the damage to Edison's hearing was severe by this time. When he had reached the age of fourteen it is said that, even if he had the means, it would have been virtually impossible for him to receive a standard education. As it turned out, by the time he was fourteen he was nearly eighty percent deaf in his right ear. Imagine. Later, this was the man who did more than anyone else to change the way we listen to music! Who knows, perhaps a deeper sense of hearing may have developed in him, which is not common to those with normal ears.

He did allow himself a few moments on occasions to mourn his loss. The sounds he missed the most, he once confessed, were the sounds of birds chirping.

The accidental fire was not without further consequences. The stationmaster banned the young entrepreneur from selling his newspapers inside the train itself. From that day forward, he had to sell his newspapers on the platform outside the cars.

How do you perceive negativity?

When faced with negativity or adverse events in your life, how do you view them? Is your first reaction to crawl under the bed and hide until the negativity blows over – all the while thinking it couldn't possibly get any worse? Or do you face the negative side of life with positive affirmations, knowing deep in your soul that things will get better or that things are not what they seem. There is a purpose to them happening. Either way, the laws are at work.

In fact, when you're continuing to look ahead with optimism, even when all you can see around you are negative outcomes, then you're also unknowingly acknowledging another law which is very pragmatic in nature. You're recognizing that the physical world doesn't always reflect reality. In spite of the negative appearance, you refuse to accept the appearance of it. This law forces you to reflect on the situation. "There is more to it than what appears to the eye," is your outlook.

The Law of Resonance

The world is not as it appears to you; it is how your thoughts are.

Explanation

The world is not what it appears to be, but rather a mirror to the lens of your thoughts and belief system. Your world, in reality, reflects your own personal internal makeup.

In other words, you will find evidence in your life of whatever you strongly believe in. If your outlook is that people are supportive in your endeavors, you will be surrounded by such people and support flows into your life. On the other hand, if you think that everyone is out to deceive you, you'll often encounter swindlers who'll further enhance your belief.

It immensely helps to be constantly aware that your life situations resonate with the choices you make. Every trial, every situation in life that seems painful or frustrating, has been consciously or unconsciously chosen by you in your past, to enable you to mature and learn vital lessons – lessons of tenacity, patience, perseverance, compassion, and being in harmony with life itself.

In addition to this, you also must keep in mind that the events you eventually attract in your life are those that *mirror* the deficiencies within you. When we consciously hold onto negative or self-defeating beliefs, we attract situations in life that prove those beliefs. We get evidence for whatever we believe through the situations that arise in our lives.

No incident or situation is a problem by itself. A situation is just a situation. It becomes a so-called problem, or triggers blame or complaint within us, only because we are viewing it through the lens of our limiting beliefs. The Law of Resonance acts as a wakeup call from Nature to alter direction or change perspective to see reality as it truly is. It is inherently always in favor of your highest potential. Often, a seemingly negative incident turns out to be something that triggers a dormant potential hidden within you into action.

So, when you change the lens of how you view the incidents, your positivity gives the signal to Nature that you agree with its flow to create for you. Every creation in your life occurs through your mental plane, directly or indirectly. No exceptions.

Back to Edison. To those observing young Edison, it must have appeared that he had no ambition, at least no plan to build a stable life for himself. He never appeared to outgrow his desire—or rather his need—to wander from one topic to another, gathering whatever information he could. He just kept going. It was probably all too easy to point a finger at him if you knew him at the time and say, "Look what happened. He wasn't satisfied just selling newspapers. He was making a good income doing that. He had to go and fool around with that darn chemical set. Why couldn't he have just settled for selling newspapers? What's wrong with that lad?"

Certainly, he didn't seem to explore options in any systematic way. He didn't seem to have a well-thought-out game plan. He continued, from all appearances, to haphazardly flit from one topic to the next, investigating whatever caught his eye. Even worse, some individuals may observe, it didn't appear as if he had any goals beyond asking his next question or disassembling the next piece of equipment about which he grew curious.

This may have been a unique and even effective approach to an education in his younger years, but how could this same style possibly serve an older and maturing scientific mind?

How was this young man going to make anything out of himself? Here again is an example of something that appears to be working and bubbling forth on the physical plane; but is quite different from what is actually taking place in the invisible realm of creation.

So, was it a negative consequence?

What is a negative consequence, anyway?

If you carefully observe, you may notice that Edison's being banned, has been described as a consequence of the accident, not an 'unfortunate' event.

Of course, as humans with a tendency of impatience, we would impulsively want to label this event—as we do every event in our lives—as good or bad, right or wrong. If Edison too did, he never mentioned it to anyone. However, suspend your judgment for a moment. If your mind is going there, simply smile and say, "We'll see." Because in a few moments, you really will see what Nature had planned for young Edison.

Experiencing a Technological Revolution

Without a doubt, the late nineteenth century was an exciting time to be in, especially if involved in scientific inquiry of any kind. The public still marveled at the telegraph. The speed at which the railroads alone moved both, cargo and people, amazed many. It was the fastest that man had ever traveled. And there was no better environment for Edison's naturally ever-inquisitive mind.

Many individuals have compared this rise of the industrial revolution with that of the growth of technology of the late nineteen sixties and early nineteen seventies. They have compared the burgeoning Silicon-valley of the mid-to-late twentieth century with the burst of imagination and technological achievement some sixty to seventy years before...

A very uncivil interruption

But some of the excitement of the time was about to change. Because there had been an issue the politicians had danced around for many decades—if not since the creation of the country—that was ready to burst forth on the national scene with a furious energy that few could have predicted.

It was the Civil War. Brother killing brother. Regardless of what history claims the reasons for the conflict were, there was no question that it sent many physically able young men off to fight.

The one thing you can predict about Edison's formative years is that nothing was predictable. And so, this very uncivil interruption in the country seemed to be right in line with the theme of Edison's life up to this point.

So it was with his discovery and involvement with the telegraph. It was the newest technology of the nineteenth century. While it no longer exists today, being eclipsed by the internet, email and smartphones interconnected at all times, it would be nearly impossible to describe how the telegraph revolutionized communications.

It increased the speed of relaying information, especially news from one end of the country to the other. In fact, it could deliver messages so quickly that barely a city or town in the United States could claim it was completely isolated—especially if it had a railway station.

But now, three events were about to coincide that would change Edison's life forever. They include the growing need for telegraph operators because of the Civil War, and a seemingly unrelated accident.

Edison himself couldn't envision how one incident could possibly change the course of his life. It occurred as he was selling his newspapers along the railroad. As you recall, he could no longer sell them in the rail cars, following the fire caused by his keeping chemicals on the train.

One day, when Edison was selling his papers, a young child fell onto the tracks of the railroad and in the path of an incoming train. He ran after the lad, scooped him up and got him off the tracks. Needless to say, the child's father was grateful. So grateful, in fact, that he taught Edison how to use the in thing in technology—the telegraph. This proved to be a critical juncture in Edison's life.

Pause and reflect

You will recall that when the chemicals that Edison kept in his room on the train caught fire, the railroad banned him from selling his papers inside the train. So, the only reason the young man was outside was what most individuals would label an unfortunate accident. That "unfortunate accident," though, led Edison into being at the right place at the right time. He saved the young child's life – and as a reward, gained an entry into the emerging technology of the day – telegraphy. Had it not been for the fire, one must wonder what would have happened to that child and what would have been the next turn in Edison's young career?

It is worth noting here that what you see on the physical plane and label as either bad or good may not be so. But in hindsight, the fire had a certain place in the machinations of Nature in order to get Edison to be properly placed later. We call such events as a "blessing in disguise" only in hindsight. But all events are actually a blessing in disguise. One should only be able look at an incident in that light when it appears unfavorable. You can call it Part-1 of God's will. Wait patiently for Part-2 to unfold.

When we do not pass judgment on any incident, our state of mind and the resulting happiness can remain intact. It was just another incident in a line of many. It is Nature's way of working. Since Nature is aligned only to bring the best for you, it should go without saying that every incident in your life eventually plays out in ways to benefit you. Very often, though, we lack the mental vision to see beyond the present moment. But be assured by the wondrous and unexpected ways of working of Nature.

What Edison really thought about the fire in the train car, we will never really know. Chances are, though, that he didn't believe it was "the end of the world" as some of us may interpret it. He seems to have been of a very spontaneous nature who would not dwell on happenings for long and would just get on with things. Perhaps it may have been what his parents instilled in his work ethics. Edison did seem to unconsciously have picked it up while observing his father's actions, which was that you can always start over. Regardless of any previous so-called "failures" (and it doesn't seem that this word was in Edison's vocabulary), you can always pick yourself up, dust yourself of soot from a fire, and start again.

Make no judgments on your past actions, because Nature is waiting to endow you with the best that's already present within you and waiting to unfold. If you look back, continually reminding yourself of what you've done wrong, you're going to miss the next big gift waiting for you.

Edison's next adventure

Armed with his newly acquired skills, Edison decided to move to his father's hometown, Ontario, Canada, to work as a telegraph assistant. As part of his job, he was to report to a main telegraph station every hour via Morse code, confirming the lines were working.

Knowing Edison's roaming mind and inquisitive nature, you probably have already figured out this was a tedious assignment for the young man. He would have to keep track of the time so that he could perform a repetitive action promptly.

Edison, quite frankly, was not equipped to deal with this small task even though every other telegraph operator seemed quite satisfied to perform it. Instead of putting all of his time toward remembering to send the message, Edison took his free time to create a machine that would do it for him (and by extension, for all other telegraph operators).

Eventually dubbed the automatic repeater, this machine sent the signal for the telegraph operator on a regular basis, even if the operator happened to fall asleep during his shift.

The transmitter and repeater for the automatic telegraph was Edison's first invention. The fact that it nearly got him fired because his supervisor found him sleeping on the job… well, just an interesting historical highlight!

He found opportunities abounding in this field. He chose to become what some have called a "tramp telegrapher." Others have referred to this as a roaming or transient telegrapher.

With the Civil War calling so many of the regular telegraphers into military service, Edison made the decision to travel from city to city wherever he was needed, substituting for the regular telegraphy employees.

His mother, surprisingly, lamented the decision. However, it seemed like a natural extension of his personality and habits. As the budding scientist traveled from one city to the next, he was able to continually satisfy his natural curiosity gathering random knowledge in his off hours.

In much the same way in which he spent his younger years, discovering almost accidentally his personal and mature method of scientific inquiry, Edison traveled throughout different locations in various cities in the country, continuing to amass practical hands-on knowledge about whatever intrigued him at the moment.

He quickly gained experience as a telegraph operator, but he was also able to satisfy his yearning to learn yet more when it came to electricity as well as other aspects of science.

He spent time in such varied places as railroad yards, machine shops, and newspaper offices. He got more practical experience with printing presses. He even worked in a jewelry shop; he worked with the latest clockwork of the day.

Higher choices - the winter coat legend

First and foremost, though, he became an expert on the telegraph machine. Every time he learned something new about it, Edison longed to learn even more. He could never quench his thirst for knowledge, especially in this area. He took apart telegraphy equipment and wouldn't rest until he could put it back together and knew exactly how it worked.

When he wasn't doing this, he spent much of his time in used bookstores. He searched for science books. He even ordered chemistry books from London and Paris.

He wouldn't be in a new town before long. The only way he could walk through his small, rented rooms was by sidestepping bottles of chemicals and various "junk" metals for his planned experiments. According to legend, Edison was so singular in mind in spending all his money buying supplies for experiments and books that one winter he went without a winter coat.

If you are sufficiently consumed by your higher purpose, sacrifices and inconveniences like even giving up the winter coat will not be a difficult decision at all. To Edison, the necessity of books and supplies for his experiments, were very clearly higher on his priority list than conveniences as a winter coat. Higher choices are easier to make and more naturally made with clarity of purpose.

The end of the war

The American Civil War ended in 1865. The following year, Edison, now nineteen, took a fulltime job with the Associated Press. This company was a newsgathering organization with reporters worldwide. The reporters would file their stories and have them telegraphed to various locations and offices throughout the globe.

Edison worked in the Louisville, Kentucky office on the midnight shift, not only receiving the latest news—much as he did when he created his own newspaper at the railroad station—but sending out news stories as well.

He told individuals he enjoyed the midnight shift because it kept his days open for him to not only read scientific journals and articles, but also to perform his experiments. By this time, he was quite steeped in his own characteristic method of scientific inquiry.

There's no telling how long Edison may have stayed in Louisville, either. The job provided him with enough money to fund his interest in science. But now, technology was about to determine another direction for the young man. He initially flourished at the position as a telegraph operator.

The early Morse code was inscribed on a piece of paper. With the advancement of technology, it was more common for the receivers to be equipped with what was known as a sounding key. This meant that a telegrapher only had to "read" the message by interpreting the sound of the clicks – the dots and the dashes.

This however, placed Edison with his hearing impairment at a distinct disadvantage. He had difficulty hearing the clicks, but needed to send and receive messages accurately… Hence, he found he had fewer job opportunities as a telegraph operator.

But before he made any new decision, another event took place at work. As you recall, he enjoyed the night shift because of the daytime it afforded him for working on his experiments. He was not at all shy about taking some of those experiments to the workplace with him.

The battery-acid incident

In an event that was reminiscent of his earlier accident in the baggage car with his chemistry set, Edison now had another accident with his chemicals while working for the news bureau.

In this instance, Edison was experimenting with a lead-acid battery. It was a relatively new device, not quite a decade old at the time. You'll probably instantly recognize it as the type of battery used in the modern automobile.

The young telegrapher spilled the highly corrosive sulphuric acid on the floor. It ran between the floorboards and spilled onto the desk on the floor below. As "luck" would have it, the desk below, onto which the acid dropped, was his supervisor's. The following morning his boss discovered the spill.

The actual conversation is lost to history forever, but it may very well have gone this way… The supervisor bellows a question the morning he walks in to find his desk charred by sulphuric acid. "Whose desk sits right above mine upstairs?" He then realizes and grabbing the nearest office courier who walks past, orders, "Bring Edison to me immediately."

Not in a position to argue, the courier skitters off to find him. Edison, who was just packing up after the night, notices the look on the young man's face. "Let me guess," he says, "My supervisor wants to talk to me."

The courier merely nods. One has to guess the courier was relieved that he hadn't to say anything more. Other employees on the floor would now have been curious. Someone would have quipped, "It's been nice knowing you, Edison." Edison merely smiles at them, but you have to suspect he knew what was coming. The moment he's on the first floor of the building, a small crowd of workers follow him—at a safe distance—toward the supervisor's desk.

"Edison," his boss begins, "do you know anything about this hole in my desk? If I'm not mistaken, it was made with… of all things… sulphuric acid?"

"Yes, sir, I do know something about that hole. It's of my doing, sir, and I'm terribly sorry about it."

"How on earth could something like this occur?"

"Well sir, it's really a matter of scientific fact that when sulphuric acid…"

"Stop," Edison's supervisor interrupts. "I don't want any scientific explanation. I just want to know if you're responsible."

"Yes sir, I am," Thomas says quietly. A corresponding hush falls over the room. Every person watching the event would have known what was coming. They also probably felt horrible. It's very likely that Edison was the best, if not among the best, telegraph operators they had in the bureau.

"You know Edison, I hate to do this because you are such a great operator and, quite frankly I know you're a genius. But I have never had sulphuric acid rain on my desk before. And I really don't want it again. So, despite your impeccable performance and your brilliant mind, I have to fire you."

The group of employees watching this would have gasped even though they knew it would happen. Perhaps several of them would have groaned, some of them even speaking up, "That's not fair, boss. Those experiments and his science make him who he is. You can't expect anything less out of him. Besides we need him."

Edison smiles. "It's okay Alex. I probably would have fired myself too, had I been in charge and that happened. I understand."

But as you have probably guessed, staying stuck in the past was not a trait of the young Edison. In fact, you've seen how on more than one occasion, unfortunate incidents turned out to be blessings in disguise.

In any event, the following year, he decided he was long overdue to visit his parents. It turned out to be an eye-opening experience for the scientist. While Edison had been busy developing a sense of scientific inquiry, creating an automatic repeater and performing various experiments (in and outside of his workplace), his parents had been quietly aging and falling into a state of destitution.

The truth of the matter was that when he returned home at the age of 21, he realized his mother, who he had once credited with being the "making of him" as a solid scientist, was slowly sliding into mental illness. His father was out of work. As much as they had supported him emotionally—and more times than not financially—Edison realized that he could no longer count on his parents to always be there for him. He realized, it was time that he needed to take control of his future, both emotionally and economically.

That meant the days of taking jobs like telegrapher's positions would no longer be suitable for him. No, he needed more stability in his life. At the same time though, he was keenly aware he didn't want to give up his love of investigating science.

Without a formal college degree or any type of solid career credentials beyond the telegraphers, he had to make solid choice with more focus in his life.

5

Boston and Beyond

Now young Edison began to recognize that his future in Ohio and the surrounding states was limited. His friends had told him that Boston was the new place to be.

Boston 1868. You could smell revolution in the air! By the smell and feel of the city as he stepped off the train, Edison knew they weren't exaggerating.

No. Not the American Revolution of some one hundred years previously. Instead, a non-violent and more expansive revolution that the United States had witnessed. The East Coast had always been the cultural center of the maturing country.

Now, some one hundred years after the founding of the country, the East Coast was fast becoming the technological and scientific hub as well. What exactly was it that Edison smelled as he watched the people hustle around the town? Was it a swirling kaleidoscope of men in suits, women in the latest dresses, a random mix of children, the smell of the latest steam engines? Or was it the Boston emerging as a hub of the invention and patenting trend that sprang up and almost carried on as "inventing business," which reflected a national emphasis placed on technical innovation. Boston—the cradle of democracy—was now transforming into one of the most important tech centers in the world.

Without a doubt, Edison smelled it and was reinvigorated; perhaps one could even say reborn by this breath of what he felt was fresh air. And he was ready to leave the Midwest behind, with his spotted history, his good memories, and the more recent bittersweet ones.

We can assume he had no regrets. Regrets of any kind don't seem to fit into his personality or his method of working. He took every opportunity he had and made the most of it. He took every misfortune, refused to label it as such, and plowed ahead, transforming that 'misfortune' into yet another step toward success. In the process, he was making a name for himself.

Edison was ready to take Boston by storm; to come to the Mecca of the technology of the time, break some rules, and create new ones.

Impossible to truly understand Edison's visible impact

No mere listing of Edison's improvements to the then current machinery, electronic equipment, and other inventions, or a list of his own innovations, could possibly do justice to the genius of Thomas Alva Edison.

The purpose of this chapter is not to impress you with the list of his inventions, but to explain how the same indomitable spirit of Edison can be yours too, when you abide by the Source laws properly, every day.

Let's just take a break to quietly note a hidden point. This is the secret to seemingly unachievable feats after long persistence. It is only in the initial stages of your journey that you need to put in an effort towards a goal. These efforts are mainly to get in tune. But once in tune, the song itself carries the singer. It is said – "Initially, you need to work towards the goal. But once in tune, the goal works on you." After this, you only need to take care to stay grounded, respecting the laws and giving them their due credit, as ego is the greatest mis-tuner of all.

Now let's continue. While we shall attempt to explain a few of the more outstanding feats that eventually transformed the entire world, it is more important to study the story of his spirit through the saga.

Don't expect to come away from this chapter with a determination to become an inventor yourself. That might happen to a few of us. But expect to walk away after having read this chapter with a determination to open up to your own potential.

Who knows what that may be? It's different for each one reading this book. In fact, right at the moment, you may not know your own potential – or in what area to direct it. And that's okay. It will come to you as you move along.

Edison's coming into his own

Boston was Edison's coming of age. During his years in Boston, he refined his freethinking style of research as he delved deeper into experimentation and experienced a series of successes.

You'll recall, as a lad, that he rejected many of the conclusions other scientists had developed because he felt their thinking was steeped in dogma. Their logic, therefore, he concluded was clouded by the need to promote their already formed worldview.

On a side note, eventually, his freethinking methodology—void of any adherence to any one scientific dogma—also is revealed in the beliefs he developed on God and religion too. He is known to have associated "Supreme Intelligence" to Nature rather than to the traditional view of God in other organized religions.

What came to the fore now was his quality of persistence that many of us admire. Its roots could have been in his witnessing his father's hardworking and resilient nature. Though not much is documented on how his father contributed to building his character, it is safe to say that he was a more silent influence. Children pick up more from observing and imbibing the vibes of the living culture around them. And his father was an entrepreneur, who held various types of occupations which required hard work and resilience. His mother on the other hand was a fearless decision=maker as well as a great instiller of self-belief in Edison. Edison states in his own words "*My mother was the making of me. She was so true, so sure of me, and I felt I had someone to live for, someone I must not disappoint.*"

All of this formed within him a character, a core that then began to express freely, standing on very strong foundations within.

Telegraphy operator by night, Inventor during daytime

Almost immediately upon descending in Boston, Edison was able to find a job as a telegraph operator. In fact, his exact position was Expert Telegraph Operator. Quite a title! And as good as he was, he reveled more in what he did during the day – experimenting. We've all heard the legend that Edison only slept four hours a night, with dashes of power naps spread throughout the rest of the day. It appears that this is true.

During this period of his career, the idea of electrical currents fascinated him, and he worked hard experimenting with them in order to improve the many innovations already being developed by a host of inventors.

A technological success that couldn't find a home

It didn't take long for Edison to invent an electric vote recorder. He had heard that both the city councils of Washington D.C. as well as New York City, were investigating quicker ways for its council members to cast their ballots. This machine provided just this.

His friend, Dewitt Roberts, bought a hundred-dollar share in the invention and took it to the U.S. Congress to demonstrate it. Instead of being met with the awe Roberts thought it deserved, his demonstration of the potential of the technology failed to impress those responsible for reviewing it.

"But, can't you see," Roberts retorted after his initial dismissal, "how much time this could save both houses of Congress?!"

"Indeed, I can, young fellow," the person responded, "but the last thing we need around here is a quick vote. A slow, lingering vote is more to the advantage of this institution. The longer it takes to take roll and cast the ballots, the more time these politicians have for maneuvering themselves, gathering new alliances and filibustering voting sessions when needed."

From that moment on, Edison vowed not to invent anything that he wasn't one hundred percent sure he could sell.

In the meantime, Edison also experimented with improving the telegraph. He discovered a way in which the machine could do more. Up to this point, it could only send one message at a time over a single wire. Edison's improvement to the telegraph enabled the machine to send multiple messages simultaneously over the same wire.

Buoyed by his ability to research in Boston, Edison decided to try his hand in another East Coast city. In 1869, he moved to New York City. It didn't take him long to see the need for yet a new invention, and it seemed as if it took even less time for him to develop it. He seemed confident that there was a need for it and a target market.

Edison improved on the stock market ticker. It used similar technology to the telegraph and teletype machines of which he was intimately familiar. His innovation to the standard machine was to have it work so that it synchronized several stock ticker transactions. He called it the Universal Stock Printer and hoped to get a minimum of $4,000 for the machine.

Imagine his surprise and delight when the Gold and Stock Telegraph Company offered him $40,000 for the innovation!

Building on this very real feeling of momentum, Edison, who was only twenty-two years old when he received this payment, quit his job and made immediate plans to establish his own research laboratory. His singular and unwavering passion towards his intention actually accelerated the process. In our normal course, 22 is where we just start our working careers (mainly because of lack of direction, intention, and focus).

The platform is set

From that moment on, he was able to spend all of his time and exert all of his talent toward inventing with few restrictions placed on him. It must have felt like a dream come true to the young man.

This stage in his life where he earned the freedom to do what he most wanted, represented a lot of the work and creativity that had gone before it in a myriad of other projects, which included even spilled chemicals and what others may have perceived as failed inventions!

Working of the Law of Focus

Just to recall here's the Law of Focus for you:

> **The Law of Focus**
>
> ***Focus on what you want, not what you don't want.***
>
> **Explanation**
>
> This law is the working principle of the results you see in your life. *What you describe is what gets prescribed in your life.* If you are ill and your description of the situation is the symptoms of the illness, it will continue to repeat and persist in your life. Instead, if during an illness, you take it as a reminder to define what you want – perfect and vibrant health, then that is the direction your focus will work towards. Because, *wherever attention goes, energy flows.*

But for our purposes, this represents the Source laws at work in Edison's life—especially the Law of Focus.

One of the reasons that many individuals may doubt the existence of such a law is that its effects are so difficult to see at times.

When an incident occurs, it is the focus of the person looking at it that brings the next set of circumstances in that person's life. There may be two people who undergo the same set of circumstances in an incident. But their reactions could be different. One focuses on what he has learnt from the incident and where the direction has to shift to align to his goals. Another chooses to focus on the external causes for the incident and whom or what to blame. He is seeking an explanation for the incident, finding fault in it. The former advances towards his goal and those are the next set of circumstances that occur in his life. The latter is stuck with a cycle of incidents that keep occurring for him to find further fault in.

Edison's path as far as we can see is straight ahead. His focus was innovation, and all incidents only provided him more insights to further innovations. What we called failures were – to him – a discovery of ways how something should not be done. Innovations need the support of wealth and hence wealth flowed into his life easily, though it was not his primary focus.

We very often refuse to attribute the real cause to an effect or outcome produced if the two are not connected closely in time and space. Many individuals prefer to refer to it as coincidence or fortune or luck, especially when they come across favorable incidents.

Others prefer to blame the lack of good things flowing to them as a matter of "bad luck." It really was nothing they did, they claim. It was more just the way the dice fell for them. A common argument from many is that they simply couldn't get a lucky break, no matter what.

Ironically, the more they believe that statement, the "truer" it becomes for them! This is because they're neglecting the Law of Focus and focusing on what they don't want by describing it. Another way of stating this law would be: **What you describe is what gets prescribed in your life.**

Years in the completion

From the time his mother marched into the one-room school-house, chastised the teacher for labeling her son as "addled" and pulled him out of school, to his first step off the train in Boston, Edison had few doubts that he would eventually succeed. Another secret to be noted here is: **What you are ready for will come to you on its own.** You have to only work on your readiness.

Much to Edison's credit, he realized that too many individuals gave up too soon, usually right before they reach a breakthrough. Had these individuals been more aware of how the Law of Manifestation worked, and its outcome being an eventuality in spite of an apparent "time-delay," they would never have stopped working toward their heart's desire.

Whether he referred to this concept as the Law of Manifestation in his private life, we'll never know. But he's quoted as saying,

"Many of life's failures are experienced by people who did not realize how close they were to success when they gave up."

Edison's first laboratory

Edison chose Newark, New Jersey as the location for his first research laboratory, which housed not only his personal experimental equipment, but also employed several machinists.

The young Edison was setting himself up as an independent entrepreneur. He formed partnerships with interested corporations, companies, and individuals. In essence, his plan was to sell his inventions to these bidders.

Edison chose a very practical method of going into business. After years of experimenting merely for the sake of the experiment, he realized that it was imperative that his products have a very real purpose. His inventions, he explained at one point, were created to solve problems or help make people's lives better.

It is said and proved that larger goals are often met with success when their motives are impersonal. Endeavors that have the larger good of humankind and are aligned to the advancement of the story of Nature, garner support from Nature itself to drive progress and foster creativity.

Notice how people whose only aim is to secure a comfortable living, remain with as much means. But the ones who aim at bettering the lives of others as well are often showered with much more than just supporting themselves. There is a hidden law at work here. **Whatever you become instrumental for, automatically flows in your life.** And not just external means, Nature provides you with the inner strength for the goals that you set, in keeping with your sincerity and passion for pursuing them. Imagine now if you were to extend this to the highest possible extent. There would really be no limit on the means you will be granted to fulfill the endeavors. Just a food for thought on how high can one aim for.

Edison's stated intention for his inventions, speak out this affirmation in practice. Nature supports the impersonal endeavors to the hilt as such goals are always aligned to Nature's own designs. Impersonal thoughts are often bestowed to open minds to take the story of Earth forward and Edison is formidable proof of this fact. Creative ideas and breakthroughs flowed through him unhindered as he let it happen with purity of intention and sincerity of purpose.

Edison's expectations exceeded

When Edison initially organized and created his research laboratory, he envisioned that the Western Union Telegraph

Company would probably be the mainstay customer. He expected for the most part, that the corporation would be the highest bidder on the innovations and inventions created by his fledgling company.

And so it was, at least for a while. Western Union would gobble up the inventions Edison offered it. There were times, however, that another firm would outbid them. An excellent example of this is the quadruplex telegraph machine. Ironically, Edison developed this machine specifically with Western Union in mind.

It is a somewhat puzzling name, coming from the function that it performs. This machine was able to transmit two signals in two different directions at the same time. Railroad tycoon Jay Gould immediately recognized the value of the innovation and outbid Western Union.

He paid Edison $100,000 for the machine not only in cash but also bonds and stock. This naturally caused some hard feelings on the part of Western Union. Perhaps that's somewhat of an understatement. This one transaction was in litigation for years.

With his ever-increasing success, Edison abided by another rule—a corollary to the Law of Creation. Very simply put: **Those who know the laws of Nature, never aim small.** This implies that those who know how these laws function, do not get affected by mere external outcomes.

Edison simply stuck to his field of work, unaffected. His goal had taken over and was carrying him now. There were bigger, more revolutionary things to follow. Over the years many individuals have described this as "taking the next logical step," or "putting feet to your prayers."

Edison, in his own practical way, said, *"Pretty much everything will come to him who hustles while he waits. I believe that restlessness is discontent, and discontent is merely the first necessity of progress. Show me a thoroughly satisfied man and I will show you a failure."* Note here the urgency within. He was not to stop moving. It was a healthy, creative discontent he was alluding to. That may be a bit harsh, but Edison certainly makes a good point.

Aligning to the Law of Creation

Are you satisfied with your life? Have you been working in the direction of the dreams of your calling, only to be disappointed on every front? Perhaps you're even considering abandoning them? You could very well be doubting yourself and your abilities right now.

Stop right there. Consider how, many great individuals, if they had stopped for want of material gains, would not be doing the things they love today. Consider what would have happened to some of our most timesaving inventions. They may never have come into being.

You can't just sit all day and affirm that good will come to you without continuity of action. You don't need to even know where you're going. The exciting part is that Nature will match your enthusiasm and send something your way for you to grasp on to.

Your job then, is to be able to recognize it. Keep your eyes open because Nature will not just speak to you in words. In fact, it seldom speaks in words. You'll receive a sign—often quite subtle—that tells you that you're on the right track.

If you listen closely enough, it will also lead you to your next step. You'll be filled with a knowing that this is the proper path for you. This sign or series of signs may manifest through the people you meet on your way to your goal. Very often, Nature sends the perfect people to aid in your goals in the proper (and perhaps only) ways you can understand it right then.

There is a fantastic way, an un-paralleled auto-system that Nature has designed for you. No man can ever design such a system.

If man were given the onus on when to do what for involuntary actions like breathing, beating his heart, he would not have survived even a day. Similarly, there are numerous aspects and areas in man's life that he needs to pay attention at their appropriate times. If man were to be given the task of working this out, it would be impossible for him to achieve what he has today.

Nature, however, has a clever system. It is called **Action Indicator**. While working out on certain aspects of life, if you happen to neglect something that needs attention right now, Nature intervenes and signals you. It might give you a backache to indicate that you have neglected exercising, before it gets worse. It might bring about a mini-financial incident to indicate you are neglecting your finances.

Nature wants perfect balance, and it takes care of you by sending these signals, indicating which area of your life you need to focus on next. Similarly, for larger goals, it guides you through indicators and opportunities it throws your way to grasp and move forward. Those who are trained and alert, decipher these and move along. Those who complain, miss the point.

You're just to keep following those signals, continually working on whatever it is you are doing. You'll know you're on the right track because Nature will constantly send you signs. Your job, of course, is to be able to recognize them. But don't worry about that. As long as you trust this way of working with Nature, you'll be alert to what it provides you.

At times it will hit you like a ton of bricks—there'll be no way you can ignore the sign. At other times, the signals sent will be subtler. They may even be in the shapes you see in clouds! How will you know for sure? Just pure intention and experience; you'll get the knack.

It comes down to a simple plan: Say yes to Nature. It may very well be that the particular circumstance didn't turn out the way you would have liked. But there is still one sure thing you can count on. Even if it didn't work out, it will lead you to the next one. Don't ever be fearful of using a clue wrongly. Nature will see to it that you eventually meet the right clues along your path.

Edison and the invention of the phonograph

Ironically, one of Edison's most profound culturally shattering inventions dealt with sound.

We've already talked about the severity of his hearing loss in his right ear. He barely had twenty percent of his hearing left. That didn't stop him, though, from developing a device that, in less than fifty years, no self-respecting teenager could live without: the phonograph. While in many ways it's outdated today, it's definitely the original ancestor of any musical conveyance we have today.

According to several of Edison's biographers, the inventor stumbled on the phonograph on the way to something else. Edison was fiddling with different ways to improve the telegraph transmitter. He ran a piece of paper through the machine. He thought the resulting sound appeared to mimic the spoken word when played at a high speed.

That led him to applying a stylus to a tin-foil cylinder, which he then rolled. It worked. He immediately requested one of his machinists, John Kruesi, to construct the apparatus. John was a Swiss-born master-mechanic who complemented Edison perfectly on such projects as the phonograph, serving as his "ears." It is said that he was able to build the machine in just thirty short hours! This is less than a standard workweek.

This occurred sometime during the year of 1877. The inventor filed a patent for the device on Christmas Eve of 1877.

The inventor of people's needs

On the development and refinement of the phonograph, Edison was once quoted as saying he wanted to see one phonograph in every home. Imagine that! Making a machine regardless of the fact they've never heard of such a machine before; which heretofore everyone lived quite well without. In fact, that was taken from a portion of the advertising campaign for the machine. He created a product that, up until then, individuals didn't realize they needed!

The patent was granted in February of the following year, and from all appearances it seemed to be an original invention. Apparently, this experiment had occurred to no one else.

Edison, though, was not just an inventor; he was fast becoming a marketing expert and a businessman as well. He wasn't about to wait for the world to discover the phonograph accidentally. The last thing Edison wanted was to have an invention that he couldn't sell, much like his electric counting ballot.

To some extent, the late Steve Jobs had a similar bent of mind. You'll recall, Jobs founded the computer company Apple. He was fond of saying that he created products that people didn't even realize they needed.

How Edison drew attention to the phonograph

Edison quickly set out telling the world what he had done. His first stop: offices of the magazine, *The Scientific American*, in New York City. He actually visited the headquarters several days before he filed for the patent. The ability of the device amazed these science-minded men. One of the editors reported on what they experienced.

"Mr. Thomas A. Edison recently came into this office, placed a little machine on our desk and turned a crank. The machine inquired into our health, asked how we liked the phonograph, informed us that it was very well, and bid us a cordial good night."

This prompted several New York newspapers to report on the invention of the phonograph. Before long, it was being mentioned in many newspapers and magazines across the country. Free publicity is always good.

Edison promptly formed a company, which purchased the phonograph for $10,000 from his research laboratory as well as paying the lab twenty percent of all sales. All in all, not a bad deal… The new company was called the Edison Speaking Phonograph Company.

It is at this point where Edison put feet to his dreams. He could have simply marketed the device on the hope and dream that people would eventually discover a need for the machine in their lives.

He wanted to ensure that individuals could imagine the many possible uses of this device. After all, it was a device that no one had ever seen. Few individuals knew exactly what it could ultimately do or exactly what to do with it.

Edison wrote about ten ways in which the machine could be valuable to people.

1. It could facilitate letter writing for the busy executive without the need for a stenographer to be present to take the dictation.
2. The phonograph could record books, which could be read to blind individuals.
3. It could be used to teach elocution, or the art of proper pronunciation.
4. Recording of music.
5. Used in music boxes and toys.
6. Clocks that could announce the time, especially announcing the time for going to meals as well as leaving work.
7. Recording of family memories.
8. Any variety of educational purposes.
9. The preservation of languages.
10. Connect it to the telephone to record calls and make permanent record of valuable information.

His insistence on continually taking that next logical step, knowing that destiny (Nature) would meet him in his efforts with an ease few of us could imagine, contributed even further to the great success his inventions met.

Persistence and consistency

These are the qualities, as mentioned before, that are often overlooked by individuals.

Instead of "sticking it out," too many individuals eventually give up. Even though they have attempted to buoy themselves with affirmations and positive, optimistic thoughts, they succumb to the negative thoughts.

Whether the negative thoughts enter their heads through their own thinking or the influence of others and society in general is not important. The vital point here is that these individuals actually listened and believed in them. That's a shame. Because many times, they are only a few steps away from success.

Edison, with his list of possible uses of the phonograph, was practicing persistence. He was helping people create ways in which to use the new device.

Do you have an idea you'd like to market? Or perhaps you need a new job and are faced with marketing yourself? It really doesn't matter what your goals are. It may be something as simple as meeting your daily budget. The key to all of these accomplishments is the quality of persistence.

You can't work at meeting your budget once a month and spend the other 29 days of the month spending wildly. You have to practice frugality all month long. The same goes for working on that novel you've been dreaming about writing. If you spend your days intending to write something whenever you get a free moment, what do you think will happen?

You probably won't have enough free moments to write that novel. However, if you set aside a certain amount of time every day where you sit down to write, you're much more likely to begin it. And if you're persistent and do it consistently, you'll discover yourself doing it every day. Before you know it, you'll go from five hundred words to a thousand to even more. In what seems like a relatively short time, chapter 1 will be completed, and chapter 2 is sitting right behind it.

More of the same

We could detail even more of Edison's inventions and innovations. Whether it was his original invention or another person's invention, he believed that whatever it was, the device could be improved upon. And if anyone was going to do just that, it might as well be he.

Think about that last sentence. If *anyone* was

going to do anything about *any* invention, it might as well be *he*. Have you ever given that thought to your own goals and desires?

Think about that company you've been meaning to start. Think of all the barriers you've placed between you and the success of the business. Why?

There is no reason in the world to think that this isn't your God-given gift: to start the business of your dreams. As long as the business is ethical and respects the rights of others, there should be nothing to keep you from establishing it and from making it the success you have always dreamed it could be.

"Where do I start?" you may ask.

1. Get clarity on what you want to do and believe first that you can do it. The clearer your statement, the more conviction you will have in it. Hold this thought tight in your mind.

2. Take the next logical step toward your goal, however small it may be.

3. As you do this, you'll soon see circumstances and situations appear. You'll be amazed at the coincidences that begin to fall into your lap. You'll meet the right people who can, at the very least, direct you to even more right people.

4. More of the same. This roughly translates in the phrase, "then continue." Practice persistence and consistency. Have faith that you're on the right

> track. As you take these sometimes seemingly small steps, you'll be able to see at least a few feet of the path in front of you. That's all you really need to see at the moment. The rest will be revealed when you're ready for it.

There is a story of a clock that was told that it had to tick 60 times in a minute. That would amount to 3600 in an hour... 86,400 in a day... 31,536,000 in a year and 1,578,150,000 times in 50 years of its intended life span. Hearing this, the clock ceased to work then and there. What a number, one cannot even comprehend!

Had it been told to just persistently and consistently tick once every second, the goal would have been effortlessly achievable. This is the power and magic of persistence

1093 US patents and an overall of 2332 patents to Edison's credit! It remained the maximum number of patents credited to any American for a very long period of time.

In the next chapter, we will see this quality at work. What does it take to bring forth an invention that changed the world in a way few others have? If not for this quality, this invention would never have happened.

6

Edison and the Electric Bulb

How deeply was Edison invested in the idea of bringing the Electric bulb as a world changing innovation?

Imagine, a world running without electricity would, within a few years, be lit up with electric bulbs. How dimension-defining this work would be! His immense knowledge and foresight into the possibilities of giving shape to a raw discovery of a phenomenon was grounded in the depth of his vision.

The hurdles were great. For decades, a practical long-lasting electric lighting system had eluded scientists. If he had to pull off what he had envisioned, it had to be backed by his conviction in it. This is what brings passion and direction, setting the Law of Direction at work.

The Law of Direction

What you think consciously and feel passionately about, will manifest.

Explanation

It means that whatever you intentionally focus your thoughts on and invest strong feelings into (whether positive or negative), will eventually become a reality in your life. The law highlights the importance of sincerity of intent in what one wants to create. The Law of Creation defines that anything is first created in the realm of thoughts.

The Law of Direction defines why we see only a few intentions manifest. Thoughts which are superficial or like castles in the air have too many contradictory and cancelling thoughts opposing them.

Note here that it is not really the words that count. It is the real intent behind the thought that counts. In other words, the level at which your thought of creation will manifest is determined by the level of the involvement of your being in it. How passionate are you? How confident are you? How badly do you want it? And are you single-pointedly focused on your goal? These matter.

This kind of mission demanded not just genius but the ability to constantly carve out the path through innumerable possibilities out of which only some led to the solution. Persistence in the dark was the key here. It demanded a constant cycle of effort and analysis to arrive at the ideal solution. So how does the Law of Direction work here?

For those who have defined their end clearly and who maintain a single-minded focus, Nature gives them direction through what seem to others as failure. It helps them refine their innovation towards what they envision. To those willing to stick it out, there is definite success.

The task was so monumental because of the clear end that Edison envisioned. Since he was committed and there was a driving inner feel that this will surely succeed, he never gave up. So, let's see how this panned out.

September 1878, Edison Research Laboratories, Menlo Park, New Jersey

"Platinum filaments," Edison said matter-of-factly. He was speaking to his associate who had asked what material he was testing in the electric lamp. "They work well enough," Edison told the man, "because the metal has a high melting point. I think we're on to something here."

January 1879

"Perhaps platinum won't work as well as I had believed," Edison told the same associate some four months later. "The continuing research shows that when you heat platinum, air is absorbed into its pores while it's being heated."

The associate raised an eyebrow. He knew that wasn't a good sign. But Edison made it explicitly clear to remove whatever doubt may have been lingering. "We all know this weakens the metal and it actually then melts at a lower temperature than what we originally believed. This is not the answer. If we use this material, the lamp won't burn long enough to be useful or economical to anyone."

His associate watched as the inventor experimented again and again attempting to find various substances that would work. The perfect material had to burn high enough and long enough to make a long-lasting electric lamp.

As one month flew into the next, Edison tried all sorts of elements, metals and more. He even documented his attempts and presented them to a meeting of the American Association for the Advancement of Science at one of the organization's conventions.

The problem began to consume him. "So, if air is the problem," he said to the associate one day, "why don't we just take the air away? What if there were no air to get absorbed through the pores?" He posed the question and expectantly waited for an answer.

"But Mr. Edison," the associate began, looking dumbfounded. He was almost afraid to speak up. "Air is everywhere. You just can't snap your fingers and get rid of the air."

"No, but if we place all of this," Edison explained patiently, waving a hand over what was sitting on the table, "in a vacuum bulb, there would be no air in there for the object to absorb." Edison gave him a sly smile as he said this.

And so, he tried placing the filament inside a vacuum bulb and heating it. He realized he was definitely onto something there. Buoyed by this small victory, he conducted even more experiments, this time involving a vacuum bulb. Indeed, he found that with removal of the air, the lamp performed immensely better. Yet, Edison still wasn't satisfied.

The hand pumps used to create vacuum still could not remove enough air. Edison had a Geissler pump made by a New York glassblowing firm and further improved on it in his lab by hiring a young glass blower from the same firm to produce an almost perfect vacuum. Air was finally not a problem any more.

He once again talked the situation over with his research associate. "The lamps are functioning fine," he said. "The main problem now is that platinum is still too darned expensive and has very low resistance to be on the electrical system I'm designing. It's close, but not there. Not yet at least."

Is it even possible?

"You know, Mr. Edison," the research aid said, "maybe what you're looking for simply can't be done." As soon as he uttered the words, he realized they were the wrong ones to suggest—especially to Thomas Alva Edison.

"Heck no," Edison bellowed, his voice echoing throughout the lab. His associate felt the eyes of all the other researchers on him now. One of them said loudly enough for all to hear, "Someone just told The Boss that he might not be able to accomplish something." The entire laboratory erupted in laughter.

The quip shattered the tension. Edison smiled. "You know, young man, some supervisors would fire employees who talked such nonsense. But you've just made sure you've got a job." Edison paused. "At least for the next several months or so. Just long enough to let me prove you wrong."

October 1879

Edison leaned back in the chair in his laboratory office. He couldn't sleep. Too many unfinished details still dangled loosely about when it came to his pursuit of a filament for the electric light bulb. The words of his assistant, Smith, several months earlier haunted his thoughts. "*Maybe what you want to do can't be done!*"

Nobody tells him what can't be done when it comes to inventions. Nothing is off limits. It was merely a matter of how long and hard a person wanted to look. And Edison was nothing if not determined. He knew in his heart of hearts it could be done. He also was positive that it was his mission to discover it.

In fact, in some ways, he thought, perhaps this is what he had been preparing for—or rather, being prepared for—all of his life. What if, he mused, allowing his mind to wander for just a few moments, if he were the one specifically designated by some greater power? What would happen then if he didn't find the solution to this puzzle?

Those thoughts only made him more determined to push forward, regardless of the time and effort involved. In fact, in his mind, this was perfect justification for not walking away from the project. That, and firing Smith for even suggesting that there may not be a solution. He chuckled to himself. No, he would never fire Smith. But it certainly was fun to scare the young man for a few moments.

He absent-mindedly rolled a piece of compressed lampblack between his forefinger and his thumb as he was thinking all of this. Soon it was nothing more than a slender thread. Sighing at his inability to make the concept of a long-burning filament for the light bulb a reality, he happened to glance down at this inadvertent creation – the slender lampblack thread. And then, he stared at it. . . Eureka!

"That's it!" he shouted out loud, even though he was alone. He realized that the lampblack may indeed be, a better burner for the bulb if it were burned at even a higher or incandescent temperature. The answer, he felt sure of now, was to burn this to even a higher temperature.

Flushed with excitement and anticipation, Edison yelled for his assistant. "Smith, get over here right away!" Even though the hour was late, the inventor was sure his faithful aid was not far off. He was right. It seemed as if Smith appeared in a flash, violating all the laws of physics. Edison told him of his epiphany. Together they began the necessary experiments to test the hypothesis.

"It's working," he said as he watched the thread burn slowly. "Of course," he commented. "Of course, it works."

Smith looked sheepishly at his boss and mentor. He said quietly, "I'm sorry I ever doubted you, Mr. Edison." The great man laughed heartily and slapped his shoulder, "It's all right, Smith," he said, "don't tell anyone but even I had my doubts at times."

Then they continued creating a plan of attack to turn this idea and single successful experiment into a viable, working device. "More experiments need to be conducted," he said, "that's obvious and to be absolutely sure of this, we'll need to use other forms of it and different compositions of it."

He stood back from the laboratory table where he had been experimenting and smiled, "I just know this is the road we've been looking for."

December 1879

"Listen up, people," Smith said as the employees of Edison's research lab gathered. It was rumored that Edison was going to make a major announcement to his employees. It was just about a given that the experiments for the electric lamp were complete and he was now about to unveil it.

Edison walked out of his office and his employees immediately began cheering. He held up a hand requesting silence. "As you can see," he said pointing at the 25 electric lights strategically placed in the large research room, "we're ready to flip the switch to demonstrate the performance of the electric lamp."

The researchers and office staff stood amazed at first as the lights were flipped on. Their senses required a few moments to fully comprehend the importance of the moment and the brightness of all the bulbs. Never before had the lab been so brightly light.

Gasps and mumblings of wonder were heard throughout the room. Then they once again broke into applause. Again, Edison requested silence. "Now we're ready to unveil the system to the general public." he said. Then he began to outline his plan.

The public gets a preview of a brightly lit world

Edison's plans went just as he had envisioned. His enduring persistence and his ability to translate his own vision of how he wanted the public to get its first view of the electric lamps proved successful. He had decided that the Menlo Park lab should be opened to the public for a short time in January 1880. He anticipated tourists, for lack of a better phrase, to tour the plant and the several rooms, which were lit solely by the new electric lamp system.

He knew this would ensure the success of the lighting on two levels. It would give him the publicity that he needed through the news organizations. They were going to be compelled to cover an event like this. But even more importantly, Edison knew the tour through the bright plant at night would whet the public's appetite for its extension into not only public buildings, but residential homes as well.

The lab was opened New Year's Day, 1880. The public was so excited to see the lighting system firsthand, that the rail system added extra trains to its schedule. The lab bustled with interested people touring it.

Edison and Smith stood at the door. "Who would have thought," Smith said, "even with these near blizzard conditions, that so many would be willing to brave the cold for this?!"

"The world as we know it, my son, is about to change," Edison said, as he nodded at the individuals passing through his lab.

"Thanks to you, sir," Smith said.

"And you. You could have considered me a mad scientist at any time during this process and have yourself a good-paying job that perhaps would have even yielded a little more respect. But you stayed with the project and me even when it appeared bleak. Thank you!"

Smith looked at his supervisor. "Oh, but what fun would there have been in walking away?" he asked him.

Several feet away from the lab entrance, another research associate explained to small groups what they were about to experience. "As you noticed on your way into the building," he said, "the walkway from the train depot and into the building is lined with electric lighting—some twenty electric lamps.

"The room we're standing in now," he continued, "is lit as bright as daylight, thanks to the strategic placement of 25 lamps." He paused, giving the people time to truly assess what they were looking at.

"Now follow me into the office and the counting room where we have eight more lighting up a smaller area. And by the way," he said as they headed for the other room, "on your way out, be sure to look at some of the adjacent homes.

"They too are lit with electric lights. You see, businesses and corporations aren't the only ones to benefit from this marvelous invention. Soon electric lighting will replace gas lamps in homes across the nation."

It was several days following the public tours. The publicity had been excellent. The *New York Herald*, the supreme newspaper of New York City at the time, was thoroughly behind the potential of electric lighting. It opened to a vividly positive description of the new electric lamps.

Yet, Smith found Edison pacing his office the day following the tour. "What's wrong, boss?" he asked, "You're acting as if you have something on your mind? The electric lamp is a big hit. What could possibly be wrong?"

"We aren't done refining it yet, Smith," Edison replied rapidly. "It's not ready in the form that it's in."

"What do you mean? Look at this place," he said, pointing to the large research area of the building. "What could possibly be wrong?"

"Carbonized cardboard," he snapped back immediately, "that's what's wrong."

Smith stared warily at Edison, afraid to ask too many more questions. He knew Edison well enough that he was about to fill him in on the rest of the details regardless.

"We used carbonized cardboard." he said, specifically pointing to the horseshoe-shaped filament.

"Yes, sir, we did. Is there something amiss?"

"I'll tell you what's amiss. This material will never withstand the commercial use that it is going to be subjected to. I just know it," Edison said, only momentarily stopping in his pacing.

"You see, Smith, I don't believe that paper is the conductor we want. Let's go into the research area for a moment and I'll show you why." When they reached the big room, Edison directed his aid to a microscope.

"Look here," he said, as they approached a microscope. Edison took the first glimpse himself, ensuring that what he wanted Smith to see was still there. Smith looked through the lenses.

"What do you see?" Edison asked.

Smith felt like it was his first day at work with the inventor again, being tested in all the rudimentary skills. He took a deep breath before answering, "It looks like a bunch of sticks thrown about randomly. While there are small areas where these fibers are packed tightly together, there are other areas where they're spaced… wow…" Smith said, pausing a moment.

“He looked up. There really are some areas with big gaps between those sticks.”

“Exactly,” Edison said, delighted his aid could see that. “Carbon may be the answer to the problem of a long-living lamp, but it certainly isn’t going to be in this form… We’ve got to find another carbon material. If we don’t, this version of the electric lamp will be of little use to anyone.”

“What are we going to do?” Smith asked. But he already knew the answer to that.

“We’re going to find it!” Edison said loudly. Without missing a beat, he told Smith, “Gather the entire staff here in ten minutes.” Then he walked back into his office.

Ten minutes later every member of the research staff was standing together in the research area, waiting for Edison to emerge from his office. When he did, he looked serious. The joy from the previous day’s victorious public presentation was gone.

“I’m sure Smith told you part of our problem” he said. “So now, I’m placing each and every one of you on a special assignment. Smith here will coordinate the research.”

Smith looked a bit startled but did his best not to show it.

“I know that somewhere in God Almighty’s workshop, there is a vegetable growing with geometrically parallel fibers that will work for us in this lamp. Look for it. All of you. Paper, in its final form, is manmade. It’s not going to work well for our purposes.”

"Dr. Moses," he said, looking at one of his best chemists standing in the front row, "work with Smith here, please. Make a systematic study of all the literature you can get your hands on when it comes to carbon substances. Hand your findings off to Smith. Then he'll make sure everyone is testing some type of natural fiber for our purposes. You all know what we need."

With that Edison went back into his office and shut the door. The staff moved swiftly and seriously. Their boss was serious. Before long, researchers throughout the laboratory were experimenting with a wide variety of grasses and canes, including bamboo, palmetto and hemp.

After countless more hours of work being poured into the electric lamp, the winner fiber for the filament was bamboo – carbonized bamboo.

A word on the seriousness of involvement and persistence on finding the right material here. It is said that Edison wrote over 1400 letters to various local governments and agencies all over the world in quest of his inexpensive material before his search finally led to Hachiman bamboo in Japan which had the fibrous structure and durability he desired. He continued to experiment with carbonized materials, eventually testing as many as 6,000 types of material in order to make an even better filament," explains Oikawa Yoshiki, managing director of the Japan Electric Association.

Still one final test

You might have thought that opening up his laboratory that New Year's Day would have been test enough for any aggressive and imaginative inventor. Had Edison made that his final test and public display of his accomplishment, it certainly would have won over cynics who said it couldn't be done.

Edison though, was not satisfied with merely illuminating his lab and surrounding area. That's why on September 4, 1882, more than two years after the debut of his first version of the light bulb, he performed the largest test up to the time on the bulb. He arranged for 25 separate buildings in the financial district of New York City to be illuminated.

The final count eventually showed that his light bulb produced more than 1,200 hours of continuous lighting. That amounts to 50 days of lighting, 24 hours a day.

Another note on his otherworldly ability of foresight, vision and execution of details. Most know that he invented the first commercially viable electric bulb. But the innovation runs much deeper. He actually envisaged and implemented the first viable electric grid system to power not just the electric lamp, but the entire range of appliances that would require power.

The principles at work

Legend has it that a reporter had once asked Edison about his failure to create a long-lasting electric light bulb, based on the large number of substances he used prior to the discovery of the carbonized bamboo.

"I did not fail 9,999 times," he said emphatically, looking the reporter straight in the eye. "I found 9,999 ways *how not* to create a long-lasting light bulb."

Yes, that quote is possibly over-used today. It's held up as a prime example of why, very often, throwing in the towel and walking away from a project with which you're struggling, is ill-advised. Rather, wise and highly successful individuals always advise you to stick with it – never give up.

While this is good practical advice, it also elucidates your faith in Nature's ways. *"The current scene is always a preparation for the next scene to unfold."* Also, his statement was not merely a technique to stay positive. It came from deep knowing and experience. It is an affirmation of the fact that every step on the way is as essential as the last when the desired result manifests. It is a realization that every step on the journey is an end result in itself. The last step unfolds only the desired result.

Some people might say, "This idea occurred to me too." The true gift, here, however, is not that you keep that idea bottled up inside but to cherish it, work with it and see it through to full maturity, till its complete manifestation. Ideas, as revolutionary in nature as the electric bulb, are bestowed by nature to those who are ready for them. The qualities of persistence and continuity were imperative for such experimentation. Others, too, get such ideas, but few take ownership to bring them to fruition.

The level at which he owned the project was revealed when he was not satisfied when he succeeded at the first level. Once he developed the bulb, his mission statement then became, *"We will make electricity so cheap that only the rich will burn candles!"*

The Law of Creation thrives on such thoughts. The better and more powerfully you form and decree the statement, the greater will it feed the Law of Creation to bring it to fruition.

Yes, that's what Edison was charged with in his lifetime. His struggles in refining electric lighting are a stunning example of how a solid foundation of patience—a knack that is developed over time—is required to withstand the poking around needed to bring it to fruition. One needs to stay around long enough for all the possibilities the idea unfolds to bring about its complete manifestation.

What would have happened had Edison just walked away from his project on that 9,999th attempt? What if he had listened to the many voices, illustrated in our story above by his assistant that wondered if the task could even be accomplished? Would another person have eventually discovered just the right filament material?

Thankfully, we'll never really need to answer that. What each of us needs to answer, however, is what we're going to do to with our tasks at hand. Are we going to tackle our project with the persistence that Edison tackled the light bulb? Or are we going to give up after the 9,999th attempt, believing we're failures?

Here again, the Law of Influence comes to the fore. Just to recall:

The Law of Influence

People's thoughts cannot influence you unless you allow them to.

Explanation

If you fear that other's thoughts about you are negative and their thoughts about you will turn to reality, then let go of this fear. When travelling in a bus, there may be twenty who might fear an accident. But what matters is the confidence of the driver. If he is positive and unfazed, the destination will be reached safely and smoothly. If you are positive and the driver isn't, then you won't be in that bus. So, either way there is nothing to fear, and there is only one place to act—with yourself.

So many attempts at getting to the right solution would certainly have had many doubters around Edison as to whether the desired result is even possible. It however requires the depth of an inner conviction in one's own approach to eliminate doubts along the way.

Not everything magically appears to you after the first try. You didn't learn to walk the very first time you stood as a baby and took that first step. Surely, you experienced more than your share of falling. But you eventually discovered that if you initially held on to the low-lying furniture in your home, you could begin to maneuver around. Every baby figures this out and is up and walking shortly thereafter.

The same principle applies when you get a little older and your parents take the training-wheels off your bicycle. Did you really hop onto that two-wheeler and go riding off with friends? Chances are you didn't. You most probably hesitantly went up and down your driveway, making sure someone was close by; at-least for a few minutes.

Only after you gained some self-confidence and became familiar with the bicycle, did you venture farther out. And guaranteed, you probably fell off the bicycle numerous times. Did that stop you? Heck no!

So why do you think you can hop on that bicycle of life, begin to ride it for the first time in the form of developing your dream and not fall off—at least once? Why is it perfectly acceptable to fall off the bicycle while we're learning but not to fail a time or two as an adult in pursuing un-trodden paths?

Everyone who has not given up cycling has succeeded learning to balance. It is easy to see the laws at work here as one's faith does not waver much. The greater the conviction, the surer is success. This is a well-trodden path. However, the same principles apply to all situations—paths that haven't been trodden before.

A modern-day parable

The story of Edison and electric light is more than just a celebration of a twentieth century success story. It's more than just a happy ending to the tale of a lad growing up being told his brain was "addled" and he would never amount to anything.

It's a modern-day parable. Dig a little below the surface and buried within this story are lessons for each and every one of us on how the laws work.

Edison may have been a genius… But then we all know what he said about genius. He discarded any special ability of his to invent, giving more credit to the effort that went into any accomplishment—from any improvement to the telegraph machine to refining and lengthening the time a light bulb glows brightly.

It's a saying that we all know: "Genius is 99 percent perspiration and 1 percent inspiration." As you follow your God-given dream and discover your greatest potential, you'll appreciate the adage more and more.

The Law of Direction states: "*What you think consciously and feel passionately about will manifest.*"

It can't help being but this way. In other words, you must persist. You must keep your goal uppermost in your mind, with a childlike enthusiasm. Don't allow any attempts that appear to be failures cloud your thinking. Remember they are not failures.

Set sacred time aside every day to take the next logical step towards your goal. By "sacred time," you must believe it's sacred. Before you begin this period, bless it through any method you're comfortable with. You may want to meditate or say a short prayer before you begin.

Don't worry that you're setting aside such a small amount of time that you fear it might not get anything of value accomplished. At the very least, you're building discipline toward working on your goal and you're refusing to forget your dream from your consciousness. Given enough attempts, you'll see it manifesting.

Perhaps slowly at first and definitely in ways you couldn't have imagined yourself creating it. But it will happen. Look back at Edison's work on the light bulb. It took years to get from the idea he had to the final product—and he had a laboratory full of researchers and chemists and others helping him.

Always remember the Law of Focus: *Focus on what you want, not what you don't want.*

Nature has a slight hearing problem! At the very least, you might say, it has selective hearing. There are certain things it hears loud and clear. Well, pretty much everything. But there are at least two words it doesn't recognize: they are "no" and "don't."

We will now talk about Edison and his role as a businessman. It took some time before he was ready to assume this role, but when one attains expertise in one area, the same principles apply to all other areas. It was not long before he evolved from an amazingly talented inventor into an amazingly successful businessman as well. His becoming a businessman stemmed from necessity. Edison was still an inventor at heart. He recognized that complete fruition of an idea lay not just in its manifestation but also its successful adoption and consumption in everyone's life.

7

Edison – a Business Visionary

"Mr. Edison," one of his associates ventured into his private office, "there's a Mr. Edward Muybridge here to see you. He says he has an appointment, and he has a contraption with him to prove it. He says you wanted to see it."

Edison immediately jumped up, "Yes, of course, of course." Edison had been in his office, partaking of what his employees called "down time." He went off by himself to mull over the events of the day, ideas for new innovations, or innovations for existing ones. No one really knew for sure what he did in there. They just knew that he demanded a certain amount of time for solitude every day. He confessed to some of his closest associates, though, that sometimes he just liked to empty his brain of everything and start over.

"I have had my best thoughts," he told a few who he believed would benefit most from his experiences, "tucked away in a quiet room. Take time every day to escape to a quiet room if only for five minutes to have your best thoughts. It's hard to think about achieving the impossible when you're surrounded with people wanting to discuss only the possible. Escape to a quiet room today and begin to see all your possibilities."

So it wasn't without a little trepidation that his employees would knock at his office door. But this time, though, as the employee gauged his reaction, he wasn't going to get chastised for it.

Edison bounded towards the door. "Indeed, he does," Edison said to his assistant. "This fellow has what he calls a 'zoopraxiscope.'" The associate merely nodded his head and headed back to work. It was another typical day at the office.

"Wait, Mr. Dickson," Edison called him back, "I would like you to see this as well. I think we may be able to do something with this, and you're probably the go-to man to make it happen."

Edison and Dickson met with Muybridge who spent quite a bit of time explaining his zoopraxiscope – a machine with a long circular disc that held a series of still photographs. The photos showed incremental movements of a single scene. When the disc spun it gave the illusion of movement. Individuals were able to look through what were called "peepholes" and see the movement.

After the initial display, Muybridge asked Edison if he would be interested in collaborating with him. Edison deliberately walked around the machine and then politely declined, citing a few reasons.

The following day, after being locked in his office for a period of time alone, Edison emerged and asked for Dickson to join him. "I want our laboratory to tackle something along the lines of that thing that Muybridge showed us yesterday," he told him.

Dickson let out a great big laugh. "Oh, I'm so glad to hear you say that, Boss," he said, "I was captivated by that machine. I was extremely disappointed when you declined to take the project up. My mind is just reeling with different ways we can improve upon it."

"I'm glad to hear that. Let's compare notes and we'll see where that leads us," Edison said as he ushered Dickson into his office.

He sat at his desk and Dickson sat on the other side of it. "Basically," Edison began, "I envision an instrument that does for the eye what the phonograph does for the ear."

Dickson, thoroughly excited by the project, began working on it immediately. He started off by using a cylinder on which to record the images. Soon, he began to experiment with celluloid strips. Edison, knowing the project was in the capable hands of his researcher, visited Paris, checking on his electric light company in France.

Indeed, Edison's confidence in his associate was well-placed. Edison returned from his overseas trip in October 1889. Dickson had several proofs-of-concept to show his supervisor.

"I think you'll be pleased with what we've come up with," Dickson said. "And I can't wait to hear what you have to say about improving these devices." The research assistant was so excited he could barely stand still. He looked more like a child waiting to open birthday presents than an adult waiting to present a major invention.

He showed his supervisor what they later would call the Kinetograph, which essentially was the progenitor of the motion picture camera. Dickson also showed Edison the Kinetoscope, which was a version of a motion picture peephole viewer, along the same lines as the one Muybridge had brought him.

As with most of his projects now, Edison kept the rights and developed an entire industry from the ground up. By 1893, Edison had arranged for a motion picture studio to be assembled in his research complex—to create short films based on various popular acts of the day, to be used in the peephole viewers. A year later, Kinetoscope parlors sprung up in all parts of New York City. It didn't take long before similar "parlors" opened in all major cities in the country.

One day, Dickson walked past the filming headquarters on his way to Edison's office. When he got there, he found the Boss gazing out of the window. "Come in, come in,"

Edison said, "sit down. I'm just investing in a little bit of downtime." Before Dickson could state what he wanted to say, Edison asked him a question.

"Tell me, Bill," he asked, "do you ever take time out of the day or when you get home, just to enjoy the silence and get in touch with yourself?"

Dickson was taken aback by the question. "Well, now and then," he answered upon brief reflection, "but probably not often enough."

"Then you should definitely do it more," Edison encouraged his associate, "even if it's only for a few moments at a time." Edison gave a brief look out of his window again. "It helps to put everything in perspective.

"For goodness' sake, do it here in the office for several moments at a time," Edison said. "I'm not going to criticize you for it. We're in the creativity business; we need to pull from our deepest depths to keep our creative juices going. You're going to discover that some of your best thinking is done in solitude."

"Yes, sir," Dickson replied, "I'll do it more often, now that you mention it."

"Good, good, Bill. I'm glad to hear that. You know you're one of the best researchers in this lab."

"Thank you, Mr. Edison," He paused a moment then said, "I passed the studio where they create the Kinetoscope films for the peephole viewers, sir," he said. "I'm really amazed at how you can take a project and implement it from start to finish." He waited to see if Edison had anything to say in return. When all he got was a small smile, he continued, "While I was working on this project, I could envision the devices and even how they work. But I couldn't, for the life of me, see us filming in this research laboratory."

Edison turned toward Dickson and said, "I've created many inventions in my lifetime already," he said. "The one thing I've learned is that I'm good at coming up with the idea and the start of the creative process."

He leaned inward over his desk and looked at his trusted researcher. "But I also instinctively know that nothing ever becomes truly successful until you include many talented and skilled individuals to help you out. That studio you see over there," he pointed in its direction, "isn't about me. It's about collaboration with others who are as enthusiastic and excited about the idea as you are. You give them a generous stake in the outcome, and they do the rest."

He looked out his window again and said, "That frees me up to move on to the next idea that has popped into my head."

He closed his eyes and then said, "Bill, you've got talent. Lots of it. If you marry your talent and your ability to focus, there's no telling where you can go in this field. It's all a matter of singularity of thought. You need to know where you want to go, how to get there, and never let any soul persuade you otherwise. Then think about it night and day."

"Thank you, sir," Dickson said. "That means a lot to me coming from you." His associate rose to leave. "I take your advice to heart."

"Anything else?" Edison asked.

"No sir, you've done more for me than you can ever imagine. Thank you."

August 11, 1896

"Welcome! Welcome, everyone! As you're well aware, this is our first convention," Edison spoke as he stood next to the oval table, "and the Manhattan Beach Hotel has been kind enough to host us and we are truly appreciative."

Edison continued, "This is the first but certainly not the last of the meetings of managers and chief engineers of the Edison plants across the country."

In attendance were the presidents and chief engineers of such electric plants as New York Edison, of which J.W. Lieb was president and John Van Vleeck was chief engineer, as well as Alexander Dow, president of the Detroit Edison Company, and Henry Ford, that plant's chief engineer.

Following the morning introductions, orientation, and discussion about the current state of business, the group then paused for lunch. The afternoon session turned to future innovations, which would fuel the need for electricity.

The conversation naturally moved to electric cars, which were only beginning to spot the urban landscape. Van Vleeck commented, "We'll be seeing more and more of these vehicles. In fact, I'm sure it won't be long until there'll be thousands on the streets."

"And each of them," Lieb continuing this train of thought, "would require quite a bit of attention from the owners. At the very least, they'll need rechargeable batteries." The conversation paused for a moment, as they realized what that would mean for the Edison companies separately and jointly. It would naturally translate into a new market and corresponding larger revenues as more markets for electricity opened up.

Dow, though, interrupted the group reverie, when he pointed at Ford, his own chief engineer and said, "This young man here, Mr. Edison, is building his own car that is powered by gasoline."

Interest turned to Ford and his endeavors. Another gentleman began to ask specific questions about Ford's gas-powered innovation. Edison, with a child-like love of all inventions—related to electricity or anything else—cupped his ear with his hand in an attempt to hear better.

In a few minutes, the participants of the conversation changed the seating arrangement with Ford sitting next to Edison so he could hear exactly how the young engineer had accomplished this.

"Is it a four-cycle engine?" he questioned the young Ford.

"Yes, sir," the man answered quickly. "Yes, it is."

"Good. Good," he replied. Then in rapid-fire succession, Edison asked more questions. "Do you explode the gas in the cylinder itself?"

Ford acknowledged that he did.

"And do you do this by a contact or a spark?" In partial response, Ford immediately took a piece of paper from his pocket and began drawing exactly what was occurring in the engine.

"The car I'm working on now," Ford said, "my second one, will have an insulating plug with a make-and-break feature." Then Ford drew a rough diagram of what that looked like.

"Young man," Edison exclaimed, pounding his fist on the table, "that's the thing! You have it right there!" he said as his index finger jabbed at the drawing. Everyone at the table could read the excitement in his face.

"Keep it up," he encouraged the young engineer, "Keep it up. That's the thing of the future. Electric cars may be popping up right now," he said, "but they're not the car of the future." A collective gasp came over the other executives of the table. Edison let out a hearty laugh.

"Don't be so surprised gentlemen," he said, "you know as well as I do that electric cars can't stray too far from power stations. Right?"

Everyone at the table had to agree. "Steam cars won't work either. They need a boiler and fire. Not really practical there, now, is it?" Again, the individuals at the table agreed.

Then he turned to Ford and looked him directly in the eye. "But your car, Mr. Ford, your car is self-contained. Brilliant! It carries its own power plant, so to speak."

"Your car requires no fire, no boiler, has no smoke and no steam." He gave Ford a big smile as he encouraged the engineer, "You have the thing. Keep at it."

Then he leaned back in his chair and closed his eyes for a moment. While some of the gentlemen at the table were unsure what was happening, those who knew Edison best knew he was withdrawing into himself temporarily. It was his form of meditation and visualization.

It wasn't long before Edison opened his eyes, put his elbows on the table, and told his trusted executives, "Yes, I can see the success of a gas-powered carriage outstripping the success of any electric car. I can see these vehicles touring the countryside by the thousands, perhaps even hundreds of thousands." He paused, looked over at Ford, and nudged him. "You need to get geared up as soon as possible for mass production, whatever that will take."

"You know, young man," he continued, "one of the problems with many individuals is that they miss opportunities just like this one because it's dressed in overalls and it looks like hard work. I admire your hard work on this, plus working a full-time job as an engineer for my company."

"I do believe you have the '*stick-to-it-iveness*' to make this work."

He paused again, as if another thought had struck him, then said, "We'll see stations where these cars can refill on hydrocarbon fuels. They'll be able to travel long distances with little effort. Mark my words."

A casual train ride

When the convention ended, Edison invited Ford to ride in an open-air train car back to New York with him. The opportunity to discuss his car in more detail, proved overpowering for the young man. He now had the encouragement he needed to continue his work—from none other, he thought, than the man who knew more about electricity than anyone else in the world.

Much to the young engineer's surprise, their conversation, at least at that point, never returned to the topic of Ford's work on his car. Instead, they talked about current events—including the possibility that the capital that businessmen relied on to start financing various ventures, may be drying up.

Then Edison sat with his eyes closed a moment. When he opened his eyes, Edison changed the topic. "It's a darn shame," he said, "the government is involved in delivering the mail. I'm sure that Benjamin Franklin had the best intentions when he suggested it, but it's too slow and not cost-effective at all." Edison sat up a little more and became a bit more animated as he told Ford exactly what he thought the best mode of delivering mail would be.

"Private companies!" he exclaimed enthusiastically. "Think of it, my boy. Why not? The country could use at least two or three private couriers that would carry letters to residential locations as well as commercial ones."

Ford had never really stopped to consider this. "You may very well be right," he said thoughtfully.

Advice on the proper battery

Ford didn't see Edison again for two or three years. It was not until the fledgling carmaker visited his West Orange, New Jersey research laboratory looking for a solution to the battery storage issue in one of his cars.

Ford was searching for a storage battery that would provide the vehicle with enough power that he could create a starter and generator in one motor unit. He also wanted the battery to supply all the other electric needs of the car as well.

Immediately Ford, in explaining what type of battery he felt he would need, grabbed for a piece of paper to draw it out. Instinctively, Edison reached for one as well to explain what he thought would work.

When Edison realized the two were discussing the problem using "dueling diagrams," he laughed. Ford, too, saw what they were doing. Edison said, "I see we both think using the same method."

Edison provided Ford with marvelous insight and much wisdom. "Unfortunately, Henry," he said, "the generator and starter will need to remain separate. That's the only way I can see this working for you."

The primary tenet of success: Connect with the Source

What can we take away from this small glimpse into the budding friendship of Edison and Ford? For one thing, we've learned creativity can only appear when you invite it. That involves being quiet enough for it to enter.

Being busy all the time means that you haven't taken the time to empty your mind of all the aspects of your day. Everybody, whether you're an Edison or not, needs time to clear the mind and allow creativity to land lightly like a butterfly into the mind.

One of the reasons why even short periods of meditation-like time are important, is because it re-connects you to your Source, whatever you may call it. Whether you recognize it by any of the many names used for God or the higher self, it's essential that you seek this relationship. Even for a few moments a day.

We'll probably never know what Edison called this Source. But it's a sure bet his moments of withdrawing inward played a major role in his creative approach to his work. He saw opportunities to fine-tune and create from a pile of "junk" (Edison's exact term for some of the items he had lying around his research laboratory). Where most individuals would only see a pile of junk, he saw future projects!

It's undoubtedly an overworked cliché that we live in hectic, fast-paced times. And it's also true today that more avenues of distraction are vying for our attention than ever before. It's inherently getting harder and harder to find any type of quiet time to spend with yourself, as Edison did.

Yet, exactly because of this cacophony of interruptions, it's all the more vital than ever before that we do just that—spend some time every day in solitude. Of course, it's easier said than done. But it's not impossible. With a little discipline and some persistent effort, you too can be the recipient of the benefits of essential "quiet time" where you can reconnect with your Source, and become inspired once again in pursuing your goals.

So, where do you begin

You begin at the beginning! By going back to your Source. The Law of Creation states: *"Before anything is created on the physical plane, it is first created from the Source on the mental plane."* This is also one of the primary goals of meditation. The practice of meditation is a structured way to connect with the Source.

If you've never thought about giving yourself the gift of quiet time, you may want to include some basic practice of meditation into your daily schedule.

Also briefly go into "inner silence" when you believe the events around you become too loud, or if you feel as if your nerves are too frayed to continue your day.

There are plenty of resources that you can call upon for meditation practices. But remember that whatever the practice, it should take you to a state of detachment from your body and your thoughts—a state of being non-involved, where you are just witnessing any experience that is going on, with neither indulgence nor resistance. What is most important is being aware of who is silently witnessing from within, who is the source of your being. Most meditation practices stop short of this last point.

But the Source will work in your life with this practice and inspire your deeds. The most authentic sources indicate that the true goal of any meditation practice is "to successfully do nothing." So, keep it simple: Whatever your experience during any meditation practice—however magical—remember that it is secondary to witnessing the witnesser.

Remember the goal—connect with the Source* and abide in Its presence. This helps you clear off clutter in your mind and helps the free flow of whatever wants to come through you. It is a conscious effort to connect with the origin of your being. One of the chief qualities of this Source is creativity. A silent mind is always receptive to the highest ideas since all preconceived notions are put aside and the "new" is given a chance.

* To understand more about The Source, and how to sculpt a life of happiness, peace, creativity, and true fulfilment, read *The Source ...Power of Happy Thoughts* by Sirshree. Scan this QR code to order your copy.

8

An Older Edison – a Change of Direction

February 11, 1911

"Happy Birthday, Mr. Edison!"

The entire staff of the West Orange Research Lab had conspired to celebrate Edison's sixty-fourth birthday. The staff surprised their boss with this celebration. Edison had no inkling that anyone even remembered his birthday.

As the research associates and other employees stood in the main room and waited for the cake to be cut, one of them reflected, "I'm surprised we were able to carry this off as a surprise."

"Yeah, it wasn't easy from what I heard," another replied.

By the time Edison reached his sixty-fourth birthday, he had invented, invested, and innovated his way to folk-hero status, not only in the United States but throughout a large part of the world as well.

Edison had reached the pinnacle of his inventing career and had carried off a marvelously creative and lucrative business and entrepreneurial career for himself. It wasn't just the electric light bulb, but the phonograph, the entire burgeoning motion picture industry, the storage battery, his establishment of a business to build the components needed to supply electricity to the country as well as his eventual business merger to form General Electric.

Despite the long list, there were still so many more innovations, inventions, and companies he had his hands in, his mind fixated on, and gave advice on. He had befriended his chief engineer from his Detroit Edison plant years previously—Henry Ford, as he developed the first gasoline-powered car.

In turn, Ford introduced him to Harvey Firestone, who encouraged Edison to find an alternative for the use of rubber on tires. For a while, this goal consumed him. Edison tried to find another substance that would last longer and provide a smoother ride than rubber. While Edison was never successful in this area, eventually, all three of these titans of industry would forge one of the best mergers the country had ever known – a close and sincere friendship.

After the birthday festivities at the lab, Edison walked back to his office, joined by several of his most trusted associates.

"Men, as you've just reminded me so poignantly," he told them, "I'm not getting any younger. Of everything I've invented, perhaps I should have tried creating some type of fountain of youth."

"I think it's about time, fellows, that I slow down a bit. I've got a group of capable young men here on the floor that I'm confident can see beyond the limits of what is possible and get to the nitty-gritty of what most people would say was impossible. That's really all I can ask for. If you guys continue to do that, well, you all know the sky's the limit on your success."

His associates began to protest but he overrode them. "Quiet down, gentlemen, quiet down," he said, as he took his hands, palms down, and pressed down on some unseen amount of air.

"I'll still be around," he promised them, "just not quite so actively. I'm going to start by re-organizing the company itself. I have such a diverse set of businesses. They certainly do deserve to be restructured somehow."

He stopped for a beat before continuing. "One of the major changes in my life," he said, "is that I won't be as active in the day-to-day running of all of them. I will still, however, be here quite a bit. After all, the research lab is where we started and where my heart lies."

"My aim in this move," he continued, "is to maintain our market viability rather than to create new inventions at the rate we once did."

After his associates left his office, Edison spent a little more time in there, just gazing out of his window, meditating on what the future may bring. He knew that as he entered his mid-60s he should pass the torch of the intense inventive spirit to his employees. He counted several who he knew immediately would be able to carry on in his tradition.

Edison's deep thought was interrupted by a knock, albeit weak, at the door. "Yes, yes, come in," he said, a little disappointed his quiet time was interrupted. "But there will be more and more of that time, soon," he assured himself.

"Mr. Edison, Mr. Ford is here to see you," his associate announced.

Edison nearly jumped from his seat to meet his old friend, Henry Ford. Their friendship, Edison remembered in his haste to meet him, went back nearly 15 years. He recalled their first meeting at the convention of Edison plants.

"Henry, my friend," Edison said, as they shook hands and then clapped each other's shoulders. "What brings you out here to New Jersey?"

"Why, you, of course," Ford answered immediately, "I wouldn't miss my friend's birthday for anything in the world." Then he looked around. "Although, by the look of that cake, it appears I already have missed all the grand festivities."

"We managed to save you some," Edison chuckled, "Of course, if you had come much later than this, I'm betting you wouldn't even have that much cake to choose from.

"Help yourself," Edison offered.

"No actually," Ford said, "I really did come to see you, not really to eat your birthday cake." The pair walked into the office. Edison pulled a chair for himself from the far corner of the room as Ford sat in the receiving chair in front of Edison's desk. Edison, then, placed his chair next to his friend.

"Now what brings you here? Really?" he asked Ford.

"Really? Your birthday. But I'm using your birthday to make a proposal."

Edison laughed. "I know you too well, Henry," he said. "You know darn well that I'm trying to lessen my load at work, not increase it. This better not be about buying into any more businesses."

Ford laughed, not only at his friend's straightforward attitude but also at his skepticism.

"Okay, I will admit that this has a bit to do with forwarding my own business, but it has much more to do with us having a little bit of fun already. I took the occasion of your birthday to also reassess my own life a bit," he said.

"I'm in trouble now," Edison mumbled.

"Indeed, you are my friend," Ford said. "Now let's get down to business, or rather, pleasure!" Edison listened carefully as Ford outlined his plans.

"By George," Edison smiled, "now that's the best proposal I've had in years. I do believe there's not a part of that proposition I find distasteful or difficult to swallow on my end."

"Good. I was hoping you would say that. Firestone has already agreed to it," Ford said, sounding like a little boy, "You, my dear friend, were the only unknown factor and I thought I had a pretty good read on you."

A delay in plans

The initiation of the proposition had to wait a few more years, as much as these men would have liked to implement it. Little did anyone realize that events in Europe would soon be affecting not only the European continent but the United States as well.

The assassination of the Archduke Franz Ferdinand of Austria changed the entire direction of the United States. It, in fact, created a conflict that we now come to know as World War I. Then it was simply called The Great War.

Even when it came to diplomatic and political events, it seemed that Edison possessed a sense of knowing what the proper moves should be. Before America entered the war, when the conflict was confined to European nations, Edison believed that the United States should be prepared to act – in some fashion. He didn't advocate for American involvement in the war. He did argue, though, that America would be better served if the nation were fully prepared to go to war and not need to, rather than go to war, ill-prepared. Additionally, he had the foresight to see that technology would be one of the keys to the winning of the war.

At first, it appeared as if his warnings were being heeded. In 1915, he was appointed the chairman of the Naval Consulting Board. The purpose of this advisory panel was to discover a way in which the U.S. government could reach out to the sciences and unite them with the war department.

Although formally labeled an advisory board, this organization did create a laboratory for research by the Navy. So, the board did a bit more than merely advise. It didn't begin operations formally though until after the war, in 1923.

Despite his confession that just several years before the war erupted, he was planning on slowing down his research work, Edison now found himself increasing his research efforts in other areas.

During the war, in fact, he worked tirelessly researching for the navy. He concentrated on the ability to detect submarines. Unfortunately, he felt as if his discoveries in this area fell on deaf ears. His suggestions and inventions were never met with the enthusiasm he thought they deserved.

The incident of the laboratory fire

Before Ford's proposal could be initiated, a second "incident" occurred. This one would apparently affect Edison in a more personal way. His research lab in West Orange, New Jersey was gutted in a fire. According to the contemporary account of the fire in *The New York Times,* more than $7,000,000 worth of damage had been done. The newspaper also noted the fire had started at 5:20 a.m. in the motion picture filming area of the lab.

Immediately, both Edison and his wife, *The Times* reported, were on the scene attempting to quell the blaze. Unfortunately, the buildings—all ten of them—were insured for only $2,000,000.

Edison, though, made the decision that very night to rebuild. *The New York Times* included in its headline that all employees were to report to work the following day.

According to a 1961 Reader's Digest article by Edison's son Charles, Edison calmly walked over to him as he watched the fire destroy his dad's work. In a childlike voice, Edison told his 24-year-old son, "Go get your mother and all her friends. They'll never see a fire like this again." When Charles objected, Edison said, "It's all right. We've just got rid of a lot of rubbish."

Later, Edison himself commented on his decision to rebuild, "I am 67; but I'm not too old to make a fresh start. I've been through a lot of things like this. It prevents man from being afflicted with ennui." He stuck to his word and immediately began rebuilding the very next morning, without firing any of his employees.

The quality of persistence is so effective that when it becomes habitual, it nullifies any mental lethargy that would have set into any lesser mortal, causing one to brood over the loss. *Only when persistence has reached such a level does one recognize that the true reason for brooding is more due to the fear of rebuilding than any other reason.*

Returning to the proposition

It seemed like a lifetime had passed since Ford had even broached the proposal to Edison. Up to this point, they certainly had no time to act upon it. They weren't really going to get the time until the early 1920s. That was when Edison, Ford, and Firestone were finally able to put their idea into action. And what exactly was that proposal Ford had spoken of more than a decade earlier?

His idea was no business merger. Nor was it to start another bigger and better company. Why, Ford wasn't even looking for Edison's advice on any new innovation to improve the automobile.

The proposition was simply to take some time off away from the office. In fact, Ford suggested they take some time away from "civilization" in a sense. Take motorcars and roam the great American outdoors; to spend time in the splendid areas that had before now, been too inaccessible for most Americans; to spend time in solitude enjoying the company of each other. Ford had decided, in fact, that the three of them would go camping.

Today that doesn't appear to be so surprisingly brilliant. But remember, the motorcar was just reaching its own level of popularity. Many individuals were still excited to own such a unique invention. Many of those who owned them, in fact, were still looking for ways to put them to good use.

No doubt, Ford had more reason than just recreational enjoyment in mind when the idea hit him. He must have had the foresight to realize that three well-known businessmen tooling around in the still relatively new gas-powered cars would attract quite a bit of attention from the press. He must have realized that he was, in effect, planning a marketing campaign for his cars.

The motorcar would allow a family to go farther than ever before on vacation in a fashion that they could actually commune with nature through camping. The idea was a stroke of brilliance. It was at once a roving advertisement for his car and a way to enjoy some time away from work.

But perhaps, most importantly, it also was a very powerful method that bonded these three men in a friendship that to this day seems as if it came from the pages of a novel.

Throughout the decade of the 1920s, the three moguls of the industrial revolution could be seen camping in the Allegany Mountains of Western Maryland as well as other areas—many of which are now state parks. It wasn't unusual to see these men take others along with them. Perhaps their most notable companion was Warren G. Harding, President of the United States.

Edison enjoyed these times. It may have been one of the few times in his adult life that he actually took part in some form of recreation. His career up to this point had been singularly focused on his inventions and the creation of businesses. Once he began camping, though, he discovered a new delight. Once, during a camping trip through Western Maryland, he said, "I like to get out in the woods and live close to nature. Every man does. It's in his blood. It's his feeble protest against civilization."

The caravan of cars that accompanied these men was quite a sight. After all, they had to take quite a few supplies, equipment, and other necessities. And, considering the state of the fledgling car at this point, not the least bit quiet.

At one point along the way, a young lad was standing by the side of the road, having been alerted of something impressive happening by all the commotion. He had run towards the road following a path leading from his home.

He was well-rewarded for his curiosity. As he stood alongside the road, he saw the line of several cars bumping along the dirt path. Edison was driving the lead car. When he saw the boy, he abruptly stopped the car and got out. He approached the youngster.

“Hello,” Edison said. Immediately the boy recognized the folk legend. Shortly after that, Ford was standing next to the prolific inventor. “Hi there,” Ford said, now seeing his friend’s reason for stopping.

“H-h-hello,” the youngster said.

“I’m Thomas Edison.”

“Yes, sir. I know. It’s a pleasure to meet you.”

“And this is my friend Henry Ford,” Edison continued.

The boy’s eyes, which had been wide with wonder until now, grew even wider. “As in. . . the Ford car?” he asked.

“Absolutely,” Ford answered quickly, flashing a smile at him. “What’s your name?”

“David,” he said, “but my friends just call me Dave.”

“Nice to meet you, Dave,” Edison replied. “I have a question for you. Do you know of any good spots we could set up camp and just enjoy the mountains for a couple of days.”

Dave smiled. “Yes, sirs, I certainly do. If you follow the road up along . . .”

The car mogul interrupted him and gave a quick wink to his companion, “Son, it would be easier just to show us, don’t you think?”

"Well, probably," the boy replied.

"Why don't you just jump into the car with us and take us there?" Edison continued the offer.

Quickly Ford asked another question, "Have you ever ridden in a car before?"

The boy's face lit up. "No, sir, I haven't. Only one person in the area has a car and I've only seen it a couple of times. It sure looks swell though."

"I assure you, son," Ford said, "it is swell. It's also swell to ride in. If you take us to this camping spot you know, we'll drive you back up here if you'd like."

"You don't need to go through all that trouble, sir," he began, "I'm used to hiking around here."

"No trouble at all. You may be used to hiking but how often do you get the chance to ride in a car? You might as well make the most of it."

The industrialists could tell the boy was considering the offer. Ford started walking back to the car and gave Dave a wave, "Come on."

Dave ran on ahead of them.

As promised, the spot Dave had in mind was extraordinary in many ways – close to a fresh spring for water, a nice clearing to build a campfire and raise a couple of tents. But most of all, it was breathtakingly beautiful. Edison and Ford simply stood there a few moments taking in the magnificent panoramic view of the mountains.

"What do you think?" David asked.

"I do believe that it is without a doubt, one of the most gorgeous sites we've ever camped on."

"Well, I'm glad I could be of help," Dave said. Edison could tell he feared overstaying his welcome. Ford must have felt the same way. "Let me drive you back to the spot you were at," he offered.

Before Dave had a chance to protest the carmaker had already hopped into the vehicle. "And son," Edison called after them, "if you get a chance tomorrow, why don't you stop by to visit? We'll probably be making some type of breakfast in the morning. You can come and join us."

Dave gave Edison a large grin. "Really?"

"Really."

The next morning Dave was back and even helped cook breakfast. As they were eating, the young boy asked, "Mr. Edison, may I ask you a question?"

Edison nodded and Dave continued, "Is it true what they said, about what you had said regarding the light bulb?"

"Depends on what you heard."

"That you didn't fail 9,999 times at finding the right substance, but discovered that many ways that it didn't work?"

Ford laughed. "It does seem a little overly optimistic, now, doesn't it?"

Edison took a bite of his egg. "Overly optimistic or not, that's exactly what I said."

Dave sat there in thoughtful silence. "I wonder if I could ever become an inventor or a car maker like you two."

Edison didn't hesitate one moment. "Of course you can, Dave."

"I don't know, my teachers don't think I'm that smart."

"Mine didn't either," Edison offered quickly.

"They didn't?" Dave asked.

"No, they didn't. But they don't have to think you're smart. The only thing that really matters is that you believe you're smart enough. And you never allow yourself to think otherwise."

Dave continued to sit thoughtfully. Edison then told him, "I'm going to let you in on a little secret. If we did all the things we are capable of, we would literally astound ourselves. And that applies to you, as well. You are far more talented than you'll ever know."

Edison sat thoughtfully for a moment and closed his eyes. Ford knew the pose well. He knew his friend was making full use of a reflective moment. When he opened his eyes, he said, "Now I have a grand idea. After we do these dishes, why don't we go down to that stream. Mr. Ford and I play this game when we're out camping together, sometimes."

The two adults looked at each other, Ford knew exactly where his friend was headed. "I noticed yesterday before we turned in to bed, that there's an old mill not far down there."

"Yes, sir, there is," the youngster said. "Why?"

"Mr. Ford and I were thinking about damming up the river not far upstream from there. We do this quite a bit when we go camping. Then we figure out what the power output of the mill would be. If you're interested in inventing or making something one day, you might like to learn how to do this."

"Oh, yes sir, I would," Dave looked at both Edison and Ford, "that would be just swell if you would teach me. I'll do my best to learn it. I promise."

"I have no doubt you'll pick this up quickly," he said. "It's not difficult at all. And then imagine going back to school and showing other kids—and even perhaps a few teachers."

"I would love that, sir," Dave answered excitedly.

As they dammed up the river and the two industrialists began showing the young lad how to calculate the potential power output of the mill, Edison stopped. He sat down and once again closed his eyes.

"He's thinking, isn't he?" the boy whispered to Ford.

"Yes, he is." Ford smiled. "And he gets some of his best ideas when he sits quietly like that. It's something we all need to do more often."

After camping

Eventually, the camping trips subsided as Edison's health grew increasingly worse. He had been diabetic for quite a while. The inventor had an estate in Florida. In 1916, Ford had the chance to buy the seven-bedroom home next door to his friend. He pounced at the opportunity. A wooden fence separated the two yards. Once the Ford family moved next door, though, the gate of the fence was continuously open. The two families called this "the friendship gate."

They truly became inseparable during this period. Eventually, Edison found himself confined to a wheelchair. That may have slowed some individuals down, but it did nothing to deter these two men to invent an ingenious—and childishly impish—way to spend their time. Ford purchased his own wheelchair, even though he physically didn't need one.

Ford and Edison would roam through their back yards, both in wheelchairs, racing and simply enjoying each other's company.

Abundance – wisdom spinning full circle

It seems that if you live long enough, you experience a complete cycle of life's wisdom. For most of us as we were growing up, it might have been difficult to recognize words of wisdom when we heard it, when our parents or other important adults in our life tried to impart them.

If we, at the very least, recognized their importance, then we would store them away and make them one of our templates by which to live and act. Then again, perhaps if at an early age, someone would have said, "This is wisdom; heed it now," we would have tossed it out the window without even slightly examining it.

The fact that in Edison's later years, when he was slowing down a bit, he was able to pass on these potentially life-altering nuggets of wisdom, is commendable.

Indeed, throughout his life he let abundance flow in his life. Be it knowledge or wealth, these only grew, with Edison sharing them with everyone that touched his life. Sure, that didn't mean he didn't have his share of apparent tragic occurrences, both personal and professional. But when viewed by a progressive mind, these are not tragic but enhancing events in one's life. On the point of sharing, think back at how happy Edison must have been when he was helping Ford work out the details of his gasoline engine for his motorcars.

Being a cause for the happiness of others naturally lets free flow into your life too. It brings about a sense of fulfillment that only makes man want to give more.

The Law of Abundance

There is an abundance of everything for everyone.

Explanation

This is Nature's way. It can also be called the law of free flow. Nature's way of working is described in a corollary to this law: *You naturally progress towards your higher potential and better life, unless and until you do not put blocks through your own thoughts.*

So, the only obstacle is thought blocks of your own belief system, which are also known as core thoughts. If your core thought is that money is hard to come by and requires tremendous hard work, then things will actually manifest only after great struggle on your part owing to this core belief.

Where there is no obstruction, everything flows freely. So, all that is needed is clarity about what you want and recognizing and releasing your obstructive core thoughts from your belief system.

Another corollary, very relevant to Edison's life, is: *Whatever you become a cause for, easily and abundantly flows into your life.* Edison's society-altering innovations needed the framework of industry to flourish and spread in the world and so all the wealth and associated infrastructure, flowed into his life.

From happiness to health, from success to wealth, from spontaneity to creativity, from love to self-belief, and everything else this generous Nature has to offer, you don't have to worry about encountering a lack of anything.

This is a truth that many of us have never learned, because from all general appearances, it's a difficult fact to accept. But the truth of the matter is that there is enough—more than enough—of everything anyone could possibly want in the universe. And each of us is connected to the same source that can provide us with this infinite abundance.

In a similar vein, Nature supplies us with all of our needs. It's just a matter of us recognizing that we're being given exactly what we need at any given moment in our lives. The question really becomes a matter of how much we're willing to receive. Because as long as we're saying yes, Nature is cooperating with us, showering its riches in all forms upon us.

Imagine everyone connected to the universe through the channel of the mind. Through this channel of thoughts and desires, whatever one needs is flowing into their lives. But when a negative thought enters the channel, it acts as a pebble in this channel. This pebble creates a tiny obstacle in the flow. If more and more negative thoughts are entertained, they collect and choke the pipeline. The flow then becomes a trickle.

Success is inherent in our Divine Plan; all we need to do is become receptive by removing our negative blocks. The flow naturally resumes.

Despite his initial difficulties, Edison persisted in his experiments. His focus on inventions, born out of creative desire with an entrepreneurial spirit benefitted everyone globally and brought him immense wealth and sense of fulfillment. If you go with the flow and trust Nature, it guides you naturally towards your highest potential.

9

Edison's Enduring Legacy

"Happy Birthday again, Tom!"

The year: 1931. Edison was celebrating his eighty-fourth birthday. More appropriately, a host of dignitaries, good friends, associates, and businessmen from around the world gathered to mark the birthday of one of the most prolific inventors the world had ever known.

While Edison was in attendance and enjoyed this party as much as he could, his health had been in decline for the last few years. In fact, he had to leave the festivities before they were over because of his health.

In October of that year, Edison passed. Several days after his death, lights across the United States were dimmed for one minute in honor and memory of the Wizard of Menlo Park.

Edison, indeed, had explored his potential more than most during his life. It's difficult to tell how many other individuals he inspired to do the same, regardless of their occupation or the path they chose toward success.

In fact, if this brief biography of the man, in any way inspires you to do the same, then that's another life touched by the persistence and determination of Thomas Edison.

There are greater heights

Not each of us is destined to become an Edison, granted. But learning from Edison's qualities, each of us can certainly follow the Source laws and train our minds and bodies to be prepared for the highest. Discovering your greatest potential means aligning your life and goals with your Source beyond the mind. Edison explored and set an example for us in some of the qualities of the Source.

From within Edison, the Source explored and demonstrated the ground rules of innovation and execution.

From within you, the Source may be waiting for your preparedness to script that life that's teeming within.

The Source has infinite possibilities and designs. It operates by the unseen laws that enhance rather than restrict its expression. Align to these laws and see how It makes you the medium to express boundless possibilities.

When you imbibe the essence of the Source laws into practice as Edison did, you begin to learn where your greatest strengths lie. When you consciously practice them, you'll find that the right people and events appear before you when you need them. You'll meet just the right people at just the right time to help you reach your goals.

When your flow is uninterrupted, what you ask Nature for will appear almost before you've finished your request. Miracles suddenly show up everywhere in your life—from the person you just happen to bump into in the grocery store to waking up one morning with an amazing idea.

In Edison's own words

Edison gained profound insights into the mental principles at work in life. These insights and their power grew significantly through his keen observation of life's experiences. This is evident when you take many of his best quotes and stack them together. No longer are they random thoughts or bits of folk wisdom, but a cohesive blueprint to attain success.

Here are some of his most profound thoughts, stated in his own words. Following each thought, liberty has been taken to incorporate some paraphrasing or elaboration of his words in an attempt to make them more relevant.

1. ***"Nearly every person who develops an idea works on it up to the point where it appears impossible to proceed and then he gets discouraged. That's not the place to become discouraged."***

   Of course, if you would have asked Edison when he did get discouraged, you may expect "Never!" as an answer. Even if he ever became discouraged with his work, he never showed it. Even when the research lab in New Jersey burned, he didn't utter a word of complaint. Instead, he announced his plans to rebuild even before the embers cooled. *The New York Times* printed in the news article the following morning that all employees were to report to work that day as if it were "business as usual."

2. ***"The reason a lot of people don't recognize opportunity is because it goes around wearing overalls and it looks like hard work."***

   Edison viewed success as something you earn after you pour your passion into a project. That doesn't mean that while you're working hard, Nature is working against you. Because it isn't. Nature is more than willing to provide you with that serendipitous encounter with just the right person to help you at the moment of your need. You need to develop the knack to recognize it.

3. ***"If we all did the things we are capable of, we would literally astound ourselves."***

Such a quote can carry weight only when it comes from a person who has walked the talk. Otherwise, it is just a cliché. The insights he gained into the capabilities of the human mind, the uninterrupted flow of astounding ideas, and the miraculous results obtained when he stuck at something long enough, were enough for him to glimpse what more man is capable of. In other words, he saw infinite possibilities. He also stated: *"It's obvious that we don't know one-millionth of one percent about anything."*

4. ***"The best thinking has been done in solitude."***

There is also Archimedes who had his "Eureka" moment in his bathtub. If you, personally, have never had a moment like this, then you're long overdue to spend some time alone. But surely you would have encountered eureka moments during a relaxing bike ride home, when an idea strikes you, resolving a problem that had vexed you for long. Make space for this precious time of relaxation in solitude. It is absolutely vital.

The prolific inventor and innovator was fond of saying, *"I have my best thoughts, tucked away in a quiet room."*

5. ***"Show me a thoroughly satisfied man and I'll show you a failure."***

The quote has relevance to those who stop on the path of progress due to mental complacency which often generates a yearning to get settled. Progress is a quality of the Source that instills the yearning to explore its potential. It is a hub of creative energy.

How can you improve your life if you've settled into it and aren't prepared for change? Of course, you love your life the way it is now—a spouse, children, a nice home. But many of us are driven by forces unseen, yearnings buried deep in our hearts. We ache either for a greater understanding of the meaning of life or for the next step on the ladder of success.

We're compelled to search for more, just as the Knights of old were compelled to search for the Holy Grail. How many times have you asked yourself, "Is this it? Is this all there is?"

6. ***"Results? Why, man, I have gotten a lot of results. I know several thousand ways that don't work."***

We limit the definition of "results" to events, circumstances, and achievements that work in our favor. But in truth, what doesn't turn out as expected is still a result!

We need to look at life with more openness. When we do, we lift the veil of timidity that ails many in action. We're afraid to step out of our comfort zones and keep acting from fear of "failure." Failure is a human concept that has trapped the possibilities of those who buy into it.

7. ***"The three great essentials to achieving anything worthwhile are: Hard work, stick-to-it-iveness, and common sense."***

   If you're not willing to stick it out, you're not going to succeed. That's what Edison believed. Exhaust all possible effort to accomplish your goal.

   To drive home this point Edison stated: "*I have far more respect for the person with a single idea who gets there, than for the person with a thousand ideas who does nothing.*"

   He called this: "*stick-to-it-iveness.*"

8. ***"Many of life's failures are experienced by people who did not realize how close they were to success when they gave up."***

   You're trying to break a stone with a hammer, and it's set to shatter on the hundredth hit. All too often, people quit at the ninety-ninth strike or before. What they don't realize is that every single impact, though seemingly fruitless, is building towards that ultimate result. The message is simple: *don't stop short of your goal.*

9. ***"Unfortunately, there seems to be far more opportunity out there than ability... We should remember that good fortune often happens when opportunity meets with preparation."***

This is Nature's law: "*Whatever you are prepared for, will naturally and inevitably flow into your life.*"

You don't have to go around looking for opportunities. Focus and diligently work solely on your preparedness.

10. ***"Whatever the mind of man creates, should be controlled by man's character."***

    Fittingly, this is the last one included here for now. There are many who attain the pinnacles of success but fall from heights only because of a lack of character. Only character, founded on solid values, helps you scale peaks and stay there.

    You would've heard the quote, *"With knowledge and skill come great responsibility."* Nature floods those who are attuned to it with great success.

Certified Guaranteed to Work

You can't buy these principles, take them out of the box, and have a slip of paper fall out that decrees, "Certified Guaranteed to Work." But as long as you're willing to do your part, just as Edison did, you might as well have a written guarantee of success!

Ponder these quotes that Edison talked about and, more importantly, put into action all his life. Also, contemplate the Source laws interspersed throughout the book. Implement them in your daily life and behold how Nature responds. It's like nothing you would've experienced before.

You'll wake up to each new day with Nature bursting to bring you more than what it did, the day before.

Edison's body of work

A brief idea of the areas of work where Edison held several patents besides the electric bulb:

Printing telegraph, typewriting machine innovations, stencil pen, speaking telegraph, phonograph, phonometer, Webber meter, electric motor, vacuum pump, electromagnetic railway system, electric generator, railway signaling, telephonic repeater, telegraphy, magnetic belting, art of electrolytic decomposition, process of extracting gold from sulphide ores, electric locomotive innovations, expansible pulley, nickel plating, system of electric signaling, science of generating electricity, transmission of power, roller for crushing ore and other material, method of making plate glass, method of breaking rocks, reproducer of sound records, electric automobiles, vehicle wheel, alkaline battery, waterproofing fibers and fabrics, flying machine, sound box, projectiles. . .

Epilogue

All knowledge we acquire in life exists on three planes, each distinguished by its source, how it is gained, and its ultimate purpose.

Essential knowledge

As we journey through life, knowledge unfurls—from acquired insights and the unique truths we discover for ourselves. Our understanding evolves as we build from the information and worldly wisdom we encounter.

Science

This particular kind of knowledge focuses on systematically understanding how things work and applying that to our advantage. It forms the core of most education systems today.

This powerful system of understanding is built on a foundation of unbiased analytical thought, embracing only those truths definitively proven through experiment and undeniable logic. Practicing this knowledge cultivates a scientific approach to learning and application. Its power lies in the reliable results derived from established facts.

The wisdom of the Source

At its heart, this knowledge is about the very Source of all life, the essence of life within each of us. It's a journey that begins with the quest for the meaning of creation itself and culminates in the direct experience of Being, which is the wellspring of all creation. Unbeknownst to many, it is solely from this Source that every insight, epiphany, creative spark, and original idea emerges.

Knowing this Source brings meaning to life and everything falls into place, leading to boundless joy and contentment. The pursuit of essential knowledge, scientific outlook, and worldly wisdom continues, but now with a twist. They are no longer the ultimate goal, but powerful instruments for the Source to express itself and unfold the story of creation.

Leveraging the Laws for lasting success

We are surrounded by information on universal laws and techniques for success. Yet only a handful of individuals truly stand out, becoming iconic for their influence on the advancement of Earth's story. If these laws were just simple formulae, why do so few genuinely grasp and harness their power?

It seems impractical to remember countless "to-dos" and figure out which law applies to every unique situation. Life is full of unpredictable scenarios, and there's no fixed formula for applying these laws. This begs the question: what is the missing link in truly understanding and applying these unseen laws?

The missing link is the Source. Consider the Universe as a dynamic story, where every participant helps unveil the Source's infinite potential. Nature, too, operates within a framework of unseen laws. For humanity to become a conduit for this boundless potential, we must align and connect with this Source.

You've likely admired performances of music or dance that possess a profound, almost mystical quality. Honest artists often reveal that the act simply "flowed" through them, guided by an inner wisdom once they surrendered their conscious control. While deliberate effort can make an action mundane, letting go of control fosters true spontaneity and leads to perfection.

So, the true art of self-expression, or what we call success, lies in connecting with the Source, being constantly aware of its presence, and abiding in genuine happiness. This happiness isn't a superficial feeling; rather, it's a profound trust that all events and circumstances are unfolding precisely as they're meant to, driving the world's story ever onward.

Be aware

Look closely at your own life and reflect: What's not working for you? What mistakes are you making? And equally important, what is working? While this book offers a starting point, there's no substitute for focused, personal contemplation of your unique context. Become keenly aware of how your beliefs and choices are scripting your life.

Be connected

Regularly immerse yourself in inner silence and actively listen to your inner voice—the Source. Pay attention to what it's asking of you and guiding you toward. You can indeed practice and strengthen your intuition, and this is the way to do it.

Be happy

Even in the most unfavorable circumstances, avoid calling it unhappiness or dwelling on regret. Such situations are merely indicators, unseen announcements that your connection to the Source has wavered. Realign with the Source by accepting what's happening, trusting that it's necessary. This will bring a calm that always results in a cheerful outlook.

These are the three fundamental requirements for all the laws to flourish in your life. Understanding even one law unlocks the others, as they are all interconnected. Think of Edison: his instinctive insights allowed spontaneity to flow in his life. The results are here for all to see—his legacy of such revolutionary creations and massive body of work.

◆◆◆

You can mail your opinion or feedback on this book to:
books.feedback@tejgyan.org

About Sirshree

Author of *The Source ...Power of Happy Thoughts*

Sirshree's spiritual quest, which began during his childhood, led him on a journey through various schools of philosophy and meditation practices. He studied a wide range of literature on mind science and spirituality. After a long period of deep contemplation on the truth of life, his quest culminated in attaining the ultimate truth.

Sirshree espouses, "All spiritual paths that lead to the truth begin differently but culminate at the same point – Understanding. This understanding is complete in itself. Listening to this understanding is enough to attain the Truth." Over the last two decades, he has dedicated his life to raise mass consciousness.

Sirshree has delivered more than 4000 discourses that throw light on this understanding. He has designed a system for wisdom that makes it accessible to all. This system has inspired people from all walks of life to progress on their journey of the Truth. Thousands of seekers join in a daily virtual prayer for World Peace and Healing at 9:09 am and 9:09 pm.

About Tej Gyan Foundation

Tej Gyan Foundation is a non-profit organization founded on the teachings of Sirshree. The Foundation disseminates Tejgyan – the wisdom that guides one from self-development to Self-realization, leading towards Self-stabilization.

The Foundation's system for imparting wisdom has been assessed by international quality auditors and accredited with the ISO 9001:2015 certification. This wisdom has been presented in a simple, systematic, and practically applicable form that makes it accessible to people from all walks of life, regardless of religion, caste, social strata, country, or belief system.

The Foundation has centers in more than 400 cities and towns across India and other countries. The mission of Tej Gyan Foundation is to create a highly evolved society by leading seekers from negative thoughts to positive thoughts and further, from positive thoughts to Happy thoughts. A 'Happy thought' is the auspicious thought of being free from all thoughts, leading to the state of supreme bliss beyond thoughts.

If you seek such wisdom that leads you beyond mere knowledge, dissolves all problems, frees you from all limiting beliefs, reveals the true nature of divinity, and establishes you in the ultimate truth, then it is time to discover Tejgyan; it is time to rise above the mundane knowledge of words and experience Tejgyan!

The MahaAasmani Magic of Awakening Retreat

Self-development to Self-realization towards Self-stabilization

Do you wish to experience unconditional happiness that is not dependent on any reason? Happiness that is permanent and only increases with time? Do you wish to experience love, peace, self-belief, harmony in relationships, prosperity, and true contentment? Do you wish to progress in all facets of your life, viz. physical, mental, social, financial, and spiritual?

If you seek answers to these questions and are thirsty for the ultimate truth, then you are welcome to participate in the MahaAasmani Magic of Awakening retreat organized by Tej Gyan Foundation. This is the Foundation's flagship retreat based on the teachings of Sirshree.

The purpose of this retreat

The purpose of this retreat is that every human being should:

- Discover the answer to "Who am I" and "Why am I?" through direct experience and be established in ultimate bliss.
- Learn the art of living in the present, free from the burden of the past and the anxiety of the future.
- Acquire practical tools to help quieten the chattering mind and dissolve problems.
- Discover missing links in the practices of Meditation (*Dhyana*), Action (*Karma*), Wisdom (*Gyana*), and Devotion (*Bhakti*).

About Books by Sirshree

Sirshree's published work includes more than 150 book titles, some of which have been translated into more than 10 languages. His literature provides a profound reading on various topics of practical living and unravels the missing links in karma, wisdom, devotion, meditation, and consciousness.

His books have been published by leading publishing houses like Penguin, Hay House, Bloomsbury, Wisdom Tree, Jaico, etc. "The Source" book series, authored by Sirshree, has sold over 10 million copies. Various luminaries and celebrities like His Holiness the Dalai Lama, publishers Mr. Reid Tracy, Ms. Tami Simon and Yoga Master Dr. B. K. S. Iyengar have released Sirshree's books and lauded his work.

The Source
Attain Both, Inner Peace and Worldly success

Awaken the Power of Faith
Discover the 7 Principles of the Highest Power of the Universe

To order books authored by Sirshree, login to:
www.gethappythoughts.org
For further details, call: +91 9011013210

SELECT BOOKS AUTHORED BY SIRSHREE

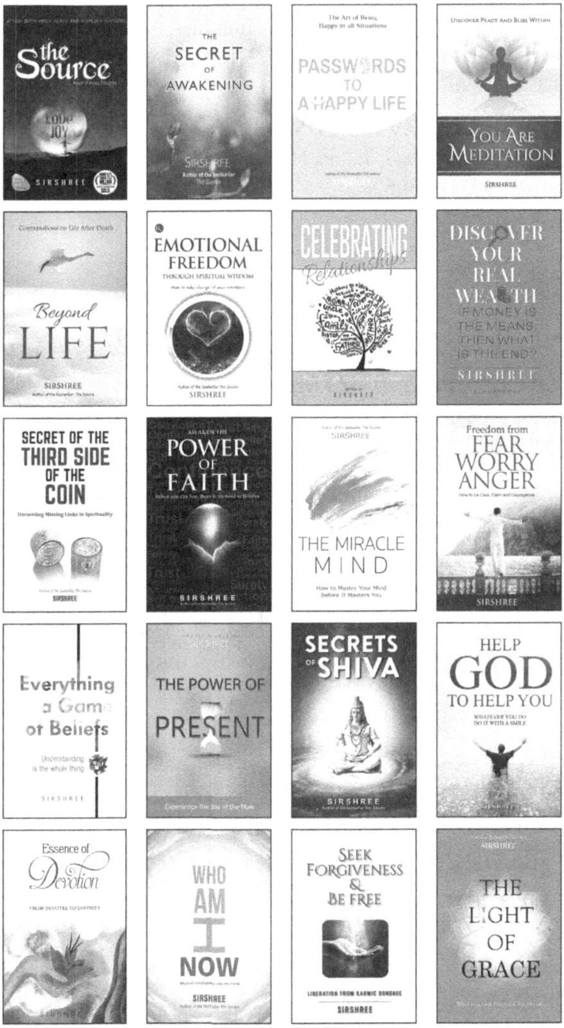

To order these and other books authored by Sirshree
Visit www.gethappythoughts.org

Tej Gyan Foundation – Contact details

Registered Office: Happy Thoughts Building, Vikrant Complex, Near Tapovan Mandir, Pimpri, Pune 411017, INDIA. Contact: +91 20-27411240, +91 20-27412576

MaNaN Ashram: Survey No. 43, Sanas Nagar, Nandoshi Gaon, Kirkatwadi Phata, Off Sinhagad Road, Taluka Haveli, Pune district - 411024, INDIA. Contact: +91 992100 8060.

WORLD PEACE PRAYER

Divine Light of Love, Bliss, and Peace is Showering;
The Golden Light of Higher Consciousness is Rising;
All negativity on Earth is Dissolving;
Everyone is in Peace and Blissfully Shining;
O God, Gratitude for Everything!

Members of Tej Gyan Foundation have been offering this impersonal mass prayer for many years. Those who are happy can offer this prayer. Those feeling low or suffering from illness can receive healing with this prayer.

If you are feeling troubled or sick, please sit to receive the healing effect of this prayer. Visualize that the divine white healing light is being showered on earth through the prayers of thousands and is also reaching you, bringing you peace and good health. You can dwell in this feeling for some time and then offer your gratitude to those offering the prayer.

A Humble Appeal

More than a million peace lovers pray for World Peace and Global Healing every morning and evening at 9:09. Also, a prayer (in Hindi) to elevate consciousness is webcast every day on YouTube at 3:30 pm and 9:00 pm IST. Please participate in this noble endeavor.

9 788198 925831

Printed at Repro India Ltd.